PRAISE FOR THE SMART STUDENT'S GUIDE SERIES

"With Understanding David Hume, Laurence Houlgate careful-ly describes and critically explains the key concepts and theories of Hume's philosophical works. He does so in a way that enables the smart student to grasp the technicalities and philosophical subtleties of Hume's reasoning. As with the pre-vious Understanding volumes, Houlgate provides to both instructors and students an excellent resource for discussing the relevance and significance of Hume's philosophy in our time."
--Stuart Silvers, Emeritus Professor of Philosophy, Clemson University

"I highly recommend this excellent introduction to Plato's dia-logues. The writing is crystal clear and accessible, with a rich analytical treatment of Plato's historical context, issues of con-cern, dialectic method and complex lines of reasoning." – (Anon. Amazon reviewer)

"It is hard to combine scholarship with accessibility, but this little volume (Understanding John Locke) does it. It is very scholarly, yet clearly written and eminently accessible to un-dergraduate students." (Anon. Amazon Reviewer)

OTHER BOOKS BY LAURENCE HOULGATE:

The Smart Student's Guides to Philosophical Classics:

Understanding David Hume: The Smart Student's Guide to *Dialogues Concerning Natural Religion* and the essay *Of Miracles*, *Of the Immortality of the Soul* and *Of Suicide.*

Understanding John Stuart Mill: The Smart Student's Guide to *Utilitarianism* and *On Liberty.*

Understanding John Locke: The Smart Student's Guide to Locke's *Second Treatise of Government.*

Understanding Plato: The Smart Student's Guide to the *Socratic Dialogues* and the *Republic.*

Philosophy of the Family:

Philosophy, Law and the Family: *A New Introduction to the Philosophy of Law*

The Child and the State: *A Normative Theory of Juvenile Rights*

Family and State: *The Philosophy of Family Law*

Morals, Marriage and Parenthood: *An Introduction to Family Ethics*

UNDERSTANDING IMMANUEL KANT

The Smart Student's Guide to
Grounding for the Metaphysics of Morals

Laurence D. Houlgate

Houlgate Books

SAN LUIS OBISPO, CALIFORNIA

DEDICATION

For Torre and Joshua

Houlgate Books
www.houlgatebooks.com

Book Layout © 2017 BookDesignTemplates.com
Formatting by Laurence Houlgate
Cover Design by VilaDesign.net

Understanding Immanuel Kant/ Laurence Houlgate. -- 1st ed.
ISBN: 9781728924502

Acknowledgements

I am grateful for the many helpful comments and suggestions of my colleague Professor Paul S. Miklowitz, who knows more than I shall ever know about the writings of Immanuel Kant. And many thanks again to Judith Perrill Houlgate for her careful proofreading of the penultimate draft of this book. I am entirely to blame for any typographical errors that might remain in the final draft.

Cover design

www.VilaDesign.net

A modest request

Thank you for reading *Understanding Immanuel Kant*. If you like this book, please write a short review on the book's Amazon.com detail page https://www.amazon.com/UNDERSTANDING-IMMANUEL-KANT-Metaphysics-Philosophical-ebook/dp/B07JHDGGJ5/

For information about other books in the *Smart Student's Guide to Philosophical Classics* series, please visit my website at www.houlgatebooks.com . And feel free to comment on my occasional philosophical ramblings at: www.houlgatebooks.blogspot.com You can also contact me at my university email address: lhoulgat@calpoly.edu

Contents

PREFACE

About the Smart Student's Guide series

In 1980 members of the faculty of the Philosophy Department at California Polytechnic State University were asked to create an introductory course in philosophy that would be required of every student as part of their general education. The department voted to adopt my proposal to introduce students to philosophy by having them read only the original texts of pre-20th century classics of philosophy. At least one of the texts selected for the introductory course had to be from ancient philosophy and the remainder could be from any book of philosophy published before 1900, provided that it is generally regarded as a classic and accessible to beginning students. We created two 11-week courses based on this model. One course is devoted to classic works in ethics, social and political philosophy. The other course concentrates on classic works in epistemology and metaphysics. The authors typically chosen for these courses were the usual suspects: Plato, Aristotle, Descartes, Hobbes, Locke, Rousseau, Hume, Mill, Kant, and several other of the "great" philosophers.

Our hope in adopting this approach to introducing university students to philosophy was that they would not only learn about the nature of philosophy and philosophical method, but they would leave the course having read and (hopefully) understood some of the great books in Western philosophy; a rare accomplishment in a university with an enrollment of 20,000 students, most of them specializing in science or technology.

Looking back over the past 36 years I believe we achieved the latter objective but fell short in fulfilling the former. Most students would begin a course completely ignorant of the nature of philosophy, its questions and its methods. This is quite understandable, especially in light of the fact that most students have no exposure to philosophy before enrolling in the university. And yet, although our beginning students studied, discussed and were tested on their understanding of several classic works, it occurred to me that a high proportion of them would leave our courses unable to give coherent answers to such questions as: "What is philosophy?" "What is the nature of a philosophical problem?" "What methods does the philosopher use to resolve philosophical problems?" "How does a philosophical discovery differ from a discovery in science?" If students who completed a beginning course in biology or psychology were not able to define "biology," or "psychology," remained ignorant about the unique nature of a problem in these areas of study and could not explain some of the methods used to solve these problems, then their teacher would understandably declare the course to be a failure.

I soon decided that I would use a standard to judge the success or failure of my courses similar to the standard used by my hypothetical biology or psychology colleague. I would evaluate my own classes as a success if a majority of my students showed an understanding not only of the central ideas of each philosopher discussed, but they could also explain the nature of philosophy, how philosophical questions differed from those arising in the sciences, and (especially) the unique methods used by the great philosophers to solve these problems.

This book is the fourth in a series of student companions to the classics of Western philosophy that attempts to achieve these modest objectives. Each book in the series organizes the central claims of each classic text with the aim of clarifying the kind of question that the philosopher is asking and the method(s) the philosopher uses in the attempt to answer that question. I make no assumptions that the kind of question asked, or the method used to answer the question will always be the same as we move from one philosopher to another. What is important is that in the attempt to clarify the questions asked by each philosopher, students will be able to identify a common thread that will allow them to say "Ah yes, this is a question that is philosophical, not scientific. It does not call for the tools or methods typically used in scientific inquiry." If questions of philosophy are not to be resolved by observational research in the field or experimentation in the laboratory, then it will be important to determine how each philosopher goes about answering the questions posed. Once again, we might be able to find a common thread that allows a student to say "There, that is how philosophers go about their work." My hope is that a critical study of the classics will show that philosophy is not after all a random enterprise in which anyone can say whatever comes into their head because they believe there is no method on which to base a rational argument.

The series title is Smart Student's Guides to Philosophical Classics. The series is organized into volumes distinguished by the author under consideration. The first volume (*Understanding Plato*) presents issues and arguments in four of Plato's early ("Socratic") dialogues and in those parts of *Republic* dealing with ethics and political philosophy. The second book is devoted to John Locke's moral and political theory in *Second Treatise of Government*. The third book is about John Stuart Mill's most famous works of philosophy: *Utilitarianism* and *On Liberty*. The fifth volume is a guide to David Hume's famous critique of the Design Argument for the nature and existence of God in *Dialogues Concerning Natural Religion*. This book also includes critical interpretations of Hume's essays *Of Miracles*, *Of the Immortality of the Soul* and *Of Suicide*. As with all volumes in the series, chapters in *Understanding Immanuel Kant* conclude with a set of questions for thought and discussion.

Although the student guides can be read on their own, my hope is that they will be read as guides or companions to the original works of the philosophers discussed therein. I certainly do not recommend the guides as a substitute for a careful reading of the classic works. Students should always read the original text before looking at this or any other companion book for commentary and guidance about what the philosopher says or implies about the nature of philosophy, the important questions of philosophy and the methods of the philosopher for answering or attempting to answer these questions.

Details about this book

Paragraphs in bold type (**like this**) are used instead of footnotes. They are mainly for clarifications, examples, comments on or criticisms of Kant.

Chapters and chapter sections in this book are headed by Arabic numerals, for example: Chapter 8, 8.1.1.

Chapters in Kant's *Grounding for the Metaphysics of Morals* are indicated in parentheses, following this book's chapter number and name, for example:

[*Grounding*, Preface]

The paragraph numbers cited in parentheses, e.g. (399). refer to passages in the James Ellington translation of *Grounding for the Metaphysics of Morals* (Hackett). Ellington's translation was selected because it is the one that is most likely to be used in contemporary English-speaking introductory philosophy courses and it is easily available at a low cost.

Quotations from authors (other than Kant) are placed in parentheses indicating the name of the author and page number quoted -- for example: (Houlgate, 18). The complete reference with author name, date of publication, book title, name of publisher and place of publication can be found in References, at the end of this book.

Please consult the Glossary at the end of the document for definitions of some of Kant's technical terms.

PART I INTRODUCTION

"[Kant's] system of thought will long remain one of the landmarks in the history of philosophical speculation." John Stuart Mill (1861)

"The Groundwork is the single most important work in modern moral philosophy." Henry E. Allison (2012)

1. ABOUT IMMANUEL KANT

Immanuel Kant did not have the extraordinary life experiences of some of the other famous philosophers discussed in this series. He did not (like Plato) witness the unjust conviction and execution of his mentor. He did not (like Locke) narrowly escape to another country to avoid capture by the political opponents of his aristocratic benefactor. Nor did he (like Mill) have to fight a lifetime of depression after growing up under the strong hand of a father who had dominated his intellectual and social life as a young man. Instead, Kant lived a quiet life in the vicinity of his birthplace, never travelling more than 60 miles from his hometown, studying and later teaching at the local university, while writing some of the greatest books in the history of philosophy.

Immanuel Kant was born April 22, 1724, in Königsberg, Prussia [now Kaliningrad, Russia], the fourth of nine children, and the oldest of those who survived. He was barely five feet tall, with a deformed chest, and constantly suffering from poor health. As a boy, he was educated in Pietist religious schools and upon graduation he began his university studies at Königsberg University. But upon the sudden death of his father, Kant's family lacked the funds to help him complete his university education. He dropped out of the university so he could support his mother and siblings by serving as a tutor to the children of three different families in a nearby town. After several years at this work, Kant had the great good fortune to meet a wealthy benefactor who was told about Kant's genius and subsequently offered to pay for his university tuition.

After graduation in 1755, Kant was offered the position of "private docent." In German universities this was the equivalent of "lecturer", with the exception that private docents received fees from their students rather than a university salary. They had to do a lot of self-marketing to build a reputation and attract enough students to sign up for their classes if they wanted to keep food on the table. Kant had no trouble attracting students, as can be discerned from the following enthusiastic account of a former student who had attended Kant's lectures on ethics:

> *Herr Kant was no mere speculative philosopher; here he was always a spirited orator who enchanted heart and feeling just as much as he satisfied the understanding. Indeed, to listen to this pure and sublime doctrine of virtue from the mouth of its creator in person, delivered with such powerful philosophical eloquence, gave a heavily delight. Oh, how often he moved us to tears, how often he forcibly shook our hearts, how often he raised our spirit and feeling... The immortal philosopher appeared to us then to be inspired with a heavenly power, and he also inspired us, who listened to him in complete amazement. His audience certainly never left a single lecture of his doctrine of morals without having become better human beings (Reinhold Jachmann).*

Kant's teaching load at the university was staggering, especially by today's standards. He taught four courses each semester, meeting his classes twenty to twenty-four hours a week, preparing his lectures, composing and grading examinations, reading student papers and hosting discussion sessions (Schneewind, Lectures, xiii). Kant taught a variety of courses, including logic, metaphysics, physical geography, anthropology, and of course moral philosophy. His students were usually younger than first year students are now. They would take the moral philosophy course as part of their first-year curriculum. "It was part of the preparation for more advanced studies of law or medicine or theology" (Schneewind, Critical Guide, xiii). To his great credit,

Kant mainly taught undergraduates, not advanced studies (graduate) students.

In 1770, after serving fifteen years as a private docent and growing fame in philosophical circles, Kant was awarded the prestigious chairs of logic and metaphysics, this time on full university salary. His lectures were now attended not only by adoring undergraduates, but by townspeople, members of the military, politicians and scholars who would travel hundreds of miles to listen to him. It was also during this long twenty-five-year period that he wrote the books that are and shall remain among the greatest works in rationalist philosophy.

Kant published his first major work, the Critique of Pure Reason, in 1781, at the age of 57. This book was the result of over a decade of reflection in which he published nothing else of significance. However, its appearance quickly established his reputation across Europe, and inaugurated a period in which Kant brought his most enduring works to print. His influential Groundwork of the Metaphysics of Morals (1785), the second edition of the Critique of Pure Reason, the Critique of Practical Reason (1788), and the Critique of the Power of Judgment (1790) all followed within the next decade. These works, together composing Kant's "critical philosophy," secured him international renown and came to dominate German philosophy. Kant continued producing significant works well into the 1790s (R. Scruton).

A notable but not well-known book on religious belief involved Kant in a dispute with Prussian authorities on the right to express religious opinions. He was charged with misusing his philosophy to the "distortion and depreciation of many leading and fundamental doctrines of sacred Scripture and Christianity" and was required by the government not to lecture or write anything further on religious subjects. In a rare show of defiance, Kant agreed but privately interpreted the ban as a personal promise to the king, Frederick William II, from which he felt himself to be released on the latter's death in 1797. After this clever sleight of hand, Kant returned to the forbidden subject of religion in his last major essay, "The Conflict of the Faculties" (O.A. Bird). At this point in his life, basking in the bright light of international fame, the Prussian government was silent.

Although Kant never married, he had many friends and led a lively social life. "Those who knew him described him as a sparkling conversationalist... He entertained frequently at home and was a prominent figure on the Königsberg social scene" (Scruton). His only impediment to a happier life was the poor state of his health. He fought back by maintaining throughout his life a severe physical regimen. His took several long walks at precise times of the day. It is said that townspeople could set their clocks by his passage through the city streets. On one memorable occasion, when no one had seen him in public for several days, they inquired and discovered that he was so engrossed in a book just published by Rousseau (Emile) that he had taken time off to read and re-read the book. For Immanuel, this is what counted as real excitement.

In the final years of his life, Kant's health dramatically declined. While under the care of his sister, Kant became increasingly antisocial and bitter over the growing loss of his memory and capacity for work. He became totally blind and finally died at the age of 79 on February 12, 1804, at his home in Königsberg.

2. KANT'S SUPREME MORAL PRINCIPLE

The title of Kant's short book is enough to intimidate a seasoned philosopher, let alone a beginning philosophy student. When Kant tells his readers that it is necessary to discuss the grounding of a metaphysics of morals before he takes on the metaphysics itself, no one would be blamed for proclaiming despair while wondering whether the rest of the book will have more mysterious words like "metaphysics" and "grounding."

Perhaps the best way to answer these questions and introduce Grounding for the Metaphysics of Morals (hereafter referred to as Grounding) is to describe how I have taught Grounding in my introductory ethics courses.

I begin by stating the supreme principle and explaining some of the technical terms therein ("maxim"and "universal law"). Next, I illustrate how the principle should be employed by applying it to one or two examples. It is only after I am convinced that my students understand how the principle is used in making moral decisions that I begin a discussion about Kant's reasoning that ultimately led him to formulate the principle.

My reason for adopting this approach is that I found that once students understood Kant's ultimate objective, this makes it much easier for them to also understand the arguments that led Kant to justify the principle. Sometimes, in philosophy, as in travel, knowing where you are going before you begin your journey can make it a lot less difficult to get there.

Kant calls his supreme principle *The Categorical Imperative* (abbreviated from now on as CI). It says:

> *"I should never act except in such a way that I can also will that my maxim should become a universal law." (402).*

A maxim is a subjective rule of acting – it is the rule on which the person *does* act, not the objective rule on which she ought to act. She won't know the objective rule until she puts the maxim to the test of the categorical imperative.

To illustrate what the supreme principle means and how it should be used in moral decision-making Kant gives several examples, the most famous of which is the example of "a man in need [who] finds himself forced to borrow money."

Suppose you are an impoverished philosophy student, always short of money, and your next car payment is due. You do not have enough money to make the payment. You know someone who will lend you money, but she wants you to "firmly promise to repay it within a fixed time." However, having just lost your job, you know that you won't be able to repay her by the designated time. What should you do? Should you tell her the truth about not being able to repay her when payment is due, or should you hide this fact and make the promise anyway?

Now suppose you take the latter option and decide to make the promise to repay the loan. Let's call this a "lying promise" because it is a promise based on the lie that you will keep the promise. Kant says that the maxim you are acting on can be expressed as follows: "When I believe myself to be in need of money, I will borrow money and promise to pay it back, although I know that I can never do so" (422).

This is a subjective rule because it applies only to you. Kant says that the moral question before you is not whether this maxim will promote your own self-interest or future welfare, but whether the maxim is morally right. The way to answer a question about whether an act is right is to transform your subjective maxim into a universal law: "How would things stand if my maxim were to become a universal law?" In this case, it would be a law that says, "Anyone believing himself to be in difficulty could promise whatever he pleases with the intention of not keeping it." It is obvious, Kant writes, that if this law were to be adopted by everyone, then "promising itself and the end to be attained thereby" would make promising itself "quite impossible." Kant means that promising would be logically impossible, not merely difficult or destructive. This is because no one would believe what had been promised him, but "would merely laugh at all such utterances as being vain pretense." (422). The end to be attained by a promise is to put oneself under an obligation to do a certain act (e.g. repay a loan). But if it is generally understood that the person making the promise does not believe he is bound to keep it, then this defeats the purpose of making a promise and having it credited by the person to whom the promise is made. The obligation to do what is promised is contradicted by the intention of the promiser not to keep his promise, if this suits his purposes. This is how Kant later puts it:

> *I can indeed will the lie but cannot at all will a universal law to lie. For by such a law there would really be no promises at all, since in vain would my willing future actions be professed to other people who would not believe what I professed or if they over hastily did believe, then they would pay me back in like coin. Therefore, my maxim would necessarily destroy itself just as soon as it was made a universal law (423).*

It is important to understand that Kant is not saying that a universal law permitting lying promises would have bad consequences. He is saying that the universal adoption of such a law is logically impossible. Something that is a logical impossibility can have neither good nor bad consequences. If I tell you that we should adopt a rule allowing married bachelors to join the priesthood, you would not respond by saying that this would have bad consequences for the Catholic ministry. Instead, you would say that such a rule could not exist because the very idea of a married bachelor is a contradiction in terms.

A student in one of Kant's classes in the winter of 1784-85, invented his own example of how reason would reject an action as immoral. His example is about theft. In a universalized form a maxim to steal whenever this is convenient could not be consistently willed to be a universal law:

> *If it were a universal rule to take from everyone what is his, 'mine' and 'thine' would cease entirely. For that which I would like to take from another a third party would take away from me* (Morongowiusz 29:609.24-27).

We should notice that the student's example is not about a contradiction in terms, as in "Married bachelors should not be allowed to join the priesthood." The concept of a married bachelor or a two-sided triangle is unthinkable. But a world or culture in which the words "mine" and "thine" cease to have meaning is certainly thinkable, for example, a world that has no concept of private property (Miklowitz). It is only in the context of private property that a maxim to steal whenever this is convenient could not become a universal law.

The Categorical Imperative (CI) is the supreme foundational principle of all morality, and (Kant argues) it should be used to determine whether any action or omission is morally right or morally wrong. Like the student who needs a loan knowing that he will not be able to repay it, Kant recommends that when in doubt about the morality of a given action or omission, we should ask and answer two simple questions: First, what is the subjective maxim or rule under which I would be acting if I were to do or refrain from doing this act? Second, "how would things stand if my maxim were to become a universal law?" Can I consistently will that everyone adopts and acts on this law (that is, is this a logical possibility)? If I can consistently will a universal law, then my action is morally right. If I cannot consistently will it, then it is morally wrong.

Before we look at other versions and applications of CI, it is now time to look into Kant's book to see how he began the intellectual journey that culminated in the discovery of his foundational principle of morals.

PART II GROUNDING FOR THE METAPHYSICS OF MORALS: COMMENTARY

3. SEARCHING FOR THE SUPREME MORAL PRINCIPLE

3.1 Kant's division of all rational knowledge

Kant begins the preface to *Grounding* by setting out the ancient Greek division of rational knowledge into formal knowledge and material knowledge. Here it is in outline form, also showing Kant's unique division of material knowledge into laws of freedom and laws of nature.

---

1)   Formal Knowledge (Logic)
2)   Material Knowledge
    a)   Laws of Freedom (Ethics)
        i)   Empirical (Practical Anthropology)
        ii)   Pure Philosophy (A Priori)
        -- Metaphysics of Morals
    b)   Laws of Nature
        i)   Empirical (Physics)
        ii)   Pure Philosophy (A Priori)
        -- Metaphysics of Nature

Formal knowledge is logic. Logic is formal in the sense that it is about the form of understanding and of reason, "and with the universal rules of thought in general without regard to differences of its objects." For example, if all A is B and all B is C, then I know that all A is C. This is a valid argument form, applying to anything that we substitute for A, B and C ("If William is purple and all purple people are radioactive, then William is radioactive"). The content (material) of A, B and C has nothing to do with the validity of the argument. Validity (and invalidity) are assessments of form, not content.

Material knowledge "has to do with determinate objects and with the laws to which these objects are subject" (387). Material knowledge is divided by Kant into laws of freedom (ethics or doctrine of morals) and laws of nature (physics or doctrine of nature). A typical law of freedom is the command "Thou shalt not lie." A typical law of nature is Kepler's law: "All planets move about the Sun in elliptical orbits, having the Sun as one of the foci." Laws of freedom are prescriptive, leaving humans free to obey or not to obey what the law commands. Laws of nature do not prescribe natural events. For example, Kepler's law (quoted above) does not command the planets to move in elliptical orbits. Instead, the law describes the observed regularity of planetary movement, allowing scientists to make accurate mathematical predictions about the location of the planets at any given time.

Because Kant's immediate concern is about the philosophical study of laws of freedom or ethics, he makes a further division of philosophy into pure philosophy and empirical philosophy. Empirical philosophy about ethics is founded on our experience of human behavior. Kant's name for this is practical anthropology. This branch of inquiry describes how people actually behave. Kant classifies it as a part of ethics because it is needed to help us make decisions about real-life ethical problems that (necessarily) will have empirical aspects.

All morals...require anthropology in order to be applied to humans, [but] must be entirely expounded at first independently of anthropology as pure philosophy... (412).

Pure philosophy, however, is founded not on experience, but on a priori principles. This directs the philosopher to study the foundations of logic, or it could direct her to metaphysics, where the study would be limited to "determinate objects of the understanding." By "determinate objects" Kant means concepts. Thus, a metaphysics of morals would have us extract moral laws a priori from moral concepts: duty, obligation, justice, rights, right and wrong.

Kant also remarks that "there is properly no other foundation for a metaphysics [of nature] than the critical examination of pure speculative reason." He is referring to the *Critique of Pure Reason*, which had already been published in 1781, and has long been hailed as one of the greatest, if not the greatest philosophical treatise ever written.

3.2 A pure moral philosophy

Kant's primary aim is to answer this question:

...whether or not there is the utmost necessity for working out for once a pure moral philosophy that is wholly cleared of everything which can only be empirical and can only belong to anthropology" (389).

There are two questions here: "Is it possible to work out a pure moral philosophy?" and "Is there the 'utmost necessity' to do this?"

What is a "pure moral philosophy"? Kant partly answers this question by saying that it has nothing in it that is empirical, that is nothing that derives from experience or observation. The empirical belongs to anthropology, not to philosophy. Anthropology or "practical anthropology" is a descriptive science based on observations of how human beings actually behave, not how they ought to behave, even though we will need empirical information to help in the application of these pure moral principles to real-life cases. For example, if we discover the logical principles on which moral duties must be grounded, these "pure" principles cannot tell us what these duties actually are, or what we should do in case of a conflict of duties.

The possible exception to this is the duty not to make a lying promise, but even this duty might come into conflict with another duty, for example the duty to save a human life (see the discussion at 8.2).

But how are we to think about moral philosophy if the supreme moral principle must be independent of the empirical? How do we answer the question "What ought I to do?" in a way that has nothing to do with how people actually behave? Kant answered this question previously when he wrote that we must look at the "determinate objects" or moral concepts of the understanding. This is exactly the sort of investigation he proposes to do in the rest of *Grounding*.

This leads to Kant's answer to the second question. There is an "utmost necessity" to work out a pure moral philosophy because otherwise laws would not be morally valid, that is, they would not be valid "as a ground of obligation" (389). To convince us of this, Kant distinguishes between precepts founded on principles of mere experience (practical rules) and precepts derived a priori from concepts of pure reason (moral laws).

3.3 Practical rules and moral laws

Examples of practical rules would be any rule that is justified by "the nature of man" or "the circumstances in which he is placed." Suppose it is said that because there is a natural desire of all human beings to pursue their own happiness, we should adopt and act on any rule or precept that promotes this end. For example, "Thou shall not kill" would be a rule that, if adopted and acted on, would bring about more human happiness than would be brought about in a society that had no such rule. This may be true, but as Kant points out, it does not explain why we have a moral obligation not to kill others. About all the rule does is show hypothetically that the universal desire for happiness can be fulfilled by restraining ourselves from killing one another. But it does not categorically say that there is a universal obligation not to kill (or harm) others.

A twentieth-century proponent of basing precepts on "principles of mere experience" is the British philosopher H.L.A. Hart. Hart writes that the rules of any society, from the most primitive to the most modern, must contain, in some form, restrictions on acts harmful to others if we are to coexist in close proximity to each other. In this respect, Hart is using what Kant refers to as "the circumstances in which [human beings] are placed." Other relevant empirical facts mentioned by Hart are the natural human desire to survive, the propensity of some persons to harm others, and the vulnerability of all humans to physical attack. These facts "afford a reason why...law and morals should include a specific content," for example prohibitions on murder, assault, rape and kidnapping (Hart, 193).

It should be obvious what Kant would say about Hart's account: these "reasons" completely fail to explain the moral obligation not to do what is prohibited by rules on murder, assault, rape and kidnapping. Hart's empirical account of the origin of the content of existing rules does not tell us why humans have a moral obligation not to kill. About all we can conclude is that if everyone was encased in an impenetrable armor (like an armadillo), making each person incapable of causing harm to one another, then there would be no need for a rule that says "Thou shalt not kill." Or if circumstances changed to such an extent that everyone's needs were fully satisfied, giving no one a motive to ever want to hurt someone else, then rules on murder and assault would likely be relics of the past.

Kant would argue that these circumstances are not only fantasies; they are irrelevant. They do not show how "Thou shalt not kill" and other rules are "valid as a ground of obligation." The only command that the rule embodies is the conditional "Given the existing circumstances of vulnerability and other facts about the nature of human beings, humans ought not to kill one another." This is a practical rule telling humans how to survive. It is not a moral law telling humans what they have an obligation to do or refrain from doing.

It follows that "all moral philosophy rests entirely on its pure part" (389). The pure parts are the laws given a priori to humans as rational beings, not merely as human beings. "The command 'Thou shall not lie' does not hold only for [humans], as if other rational beings had no need to abide by it." Moral validity must carry with it absolute necessity, and this is only to be found through an a priori investigation of moral concepts as they apply to all rational beings.

3.4 Analytic, synthetic, a priori and a posteriori.

In Utilitarianism, John Stuart Mill draws a distinction between the intuitive and the inductive school of ethics. The intuitive school holds that the principles of morals are "evident a priori, requiring nothing to command assent except that the meaning of the terms be understood" (Mill, 2). According to the inductive school, "right and wrong, as well as truth and falsehood, are questions of observation and experience" (3). About all these schools have in common is that they recognize the same moral laws and they insist that "morality must be deduced from principles" (3).

The distinction between intuitive and inductive schools is also known as the distinction between rationalist and empirical schools of ethics.

It is clear that Kant is firmly in the intuitive camp. Moral laws are not valid unless they are derived a priori from concepts of pure reason:

> "...the moral law in its purity and genuineness ...can be sought nowhere but in a pure philosophy. Therefore, pure philosophy (metaphysics) must proceed; without it there can be no philosophy at all" (390).

Since so much rests on knowledge gained a priori, it is time to pause and review what Kant means by this word, understand how it compares to other ways of knowing and how a priori knowledge relates to Kant's distinction between different kinds of judgments.

A priori knowledge or justification is independent of (prior to) experience, as with mathematics (3 + 2 = 5), tautologies ("All bachelors are unmarried"), and deduction from premises ("If Socrates is a man and all men are mortal, then Socrates is mortal"). A posteriori knowledge is dependent on (posterior to) experience or empirical evidence, as with personal observations ("All bachelors want to get married") and induction from premises ("If Mary was at the Republican rally last night, then she is probably a Republican").

Here is how Kant distinguishes between analytic and synthetic judgments:

> In all judgments in which the relation of a subject to the predicate is thought...this relation is possible in two different ways. Either the predicate B belongs to the subject A as something that is (covertly) contained in this concept A; or B lies entirely outside the concept A, though to be sure it stands in connection with it. In the first case, I call the judgment analytic, in the second synthetic. (Kant, Critique, A6–7)

For example, in the analytic judgment "All bachelors are unmarried," the predicate "unmarried" is contained in the subject term "bachelor." But in the synthetic judgment "All bachelors want to get married," the predicate "want to get married" is outside the concept of bachelor, that is, "wanting to get married" is not to be found in the meaning of the word "bachelor." The predicate ("want to get married") "is something entirely different" from that which is contained in the mere concept ("bachelor") in general (A7), and we must put together, or synthesize, the different concepts, "bachelor" and "wants to get married." This does not mean that the judgment is true. It only means that we need to look outside the concept if we want to find out whether it is true or false.

All analytic judgments are "evident a priori." One needs only to know the meaning of the word "bachelor" to know the judgment "All bachelors are unmarried" is true. It is not necessary to interview bachelors to find out whether each of them is unmarried. Indeed, if anyone announces that they have found a married bachelor, they are either joking or they are displaying their ignorance about the meaning of "bachelor."

Most but not all synthetic judgments are determined to be true or false by observation and experience. The only way one could determine whether it is true that all bachelors want to get married is to find at least one bachelor who does not want to get married. You cannot determine this by thinking hard about the concept Bachelor.

According to Kant, there are some synthetic judgments that are known to be true a priori. This includes judgments in arithmetic, geometry, the foundations of physics, and ethics. Although this claim soon became very controversial in philosophical circles (Rey; Coffa), it did provide a way for Kant to avoid the objection that if ethical judgments (e.g. "Thou shall not lie") are not analytic then they cannot be known a priori.

But classifying ethical judgments as synthetic comes at a cost because "appreciating the truth of the proposition would seem to require some kind of active synthesis of the mind uniting the different constituent thoughts" (Rey). What are we to conclude if some of us are not able to unite the thoughts "rational being" and "thou shall not lie," while others say that they are able to do this?

3.5 The search for a supreme principle of morality

Grounding (1785) is a preliminary to Kant's *Metaphysics of Morals*, published twelve years later (1797). He admits that a critical examination of pure practical reason is "not so absolutely necessary" as a critique of pure speculative reason because "human reason can, even in the most ordinary mind, be easily brought in moral matters to a high degree of correctness and precision" (301). And yet a critical examination will play an important role because the ultimate aim of a critique of pure practical reason is to seek out and establish "the supreme principle of morality." This task, Kant writes, should be kept separate from every other moral inquiry, including the promised metaphysics of morals in which the adequacy of the supreme principle will be tested by its application "to the whole ethical system." In this respect, Kant agrees with Mill that "a test of right and wrong [a first principle of morals] must be the means...of ascertaining what is right or wrong, and not a consequence of having already ascertained it" (Mill, Util., 2).

And thus, Kant has set the stage for his extraordinary attempt to prove a foundational principle a priori from concepts of pure reason.

3.6 Questions for thought and discussion

1. What are some examples of analytic and synthetic judgments? Explain why you classify your examples as either analytic or synthetic.

2. What are some examples of a priori and a posteriori knowledge? Explain why you classify your examples as either a priori or a posteriori.

3. Are there any synthetic judgments that are known a priori? Explain.

4. What is the difference between a practical rule and a moral rule? Give an example of each kind of rule.

5. How would you classify a rule that says, "If you want others to be your friend, then never lie to them"? Explain.

4. PHILOSOPHICAL KNOWLEDGE OF MORALITY

[*Grounding*, First Section: Transition from the Ordinary Rational Knowledge of Morality to the Philosophical]

4.1 A good will

Kant begins the chapter with what has become one of the most quotable sentences in the history of philosophical ethics:

> *There is no possibility of thinking of anything at all in the world, or even out of it, which can be regarded as good without qualification, except a good will* (303).

For example, intelligence is good but only under the condition that it is prevented by a good will from doing something bad and harmful. There are dictators, mobsters, con men and other miscreants who are much more dangerous because of their intelligence than they would have been without it.

Moderation in emotions and passions, self-control and calm deliberation, although praised by the ancient Greek philosophers, can also become extremely bad without the intervention of a good will (imagine the self-control and calm deliberation of a hired assassin as he does his villainous work).

Kant puts intelligence in the category of talents of the mind. Other talents are wit and judgment. They are also "good and desirable," but only if there is a good will to "correct their influence." The same can be said of gifts of nature (courage, resolution and perseverance), and gifts of fortune (power, fortune, riches, honor, health, happiness).

Kant singles out happiness, the utilitarian favorite, to show how happiness is good but only on the condition that it is coupled with a good will:

> *[T]hat well-being and contentment with one's condition which is called happiness make[s] for pride and often hereby even arrogance unless there is a good will to correct their influence on the mind...The sight of a being who is not graced by any touch of a pure and good will but who yet enjoys an uninterrupted prosperity can never delight a rational and impartial spectator. Thus, a good will seems to constitute the indispensable condition of being even worthy of happiness* (393).

Kant contends that a good will is good in itself, "not because of its fitness to attain some proposed end" but "only through its willing" (394).

4.2 Reason and will

What is "the purpose of nature in assigning to reason the governing of the will"? (395) Notice that Kant's question assumes that (a) nature has a purpose and (b) reason governs the will. These claims will not be contested here except to point out that they both require an argument, and both are highly controversial. The notion of "purpose" in (a) is ambiguous. It might refer to the purpose or plan of an intelligent being or it might simply be a colorful way of saying that events in nature occur with such regularity that scientists can make accurate predictions about the future.

The idea of reason governing the will was first put forward by Plato ("The supremacy of reason," *Republic*, 586e), but was strongly contested by David Hume who famously wrote "Reason is and ought only to be the slave of the passions" (*Treatise*, II.3.3 415).

Kant begins to answer his question by making the empirical claim that "in an organized being," (e.g. a human being), the end of each and every organ is whatever is "the most fit and the best adapted for that end" (395). Kant gives no examples, but Plato, who two thousand years earlier had made essentially the same observation, said that "[T]he function of each thing is what it alone can do or it does better than anything else" (353a). Plato used the examples of the eye and the ear. The function of the eye is to see because only it can do this. Kant would say that the end of the eye is whatever is "the most fit and the best adapted" to this end (seeing).

This brings Kant to ask about the end (purpose) of reason. He proposes two replies: either reason in a being is there to carry out the purpose of that being's happiness (preservation and welfare) or it is there to "have influence on the will," in particular "to produce a will which is not merely good as a means to some further end but is good in itself" (396).

Kant dispenses with the first alternative with the remark that "nature would have hit upon a very poor arrangement" in having the faculty of reason carry out the purpose of promoting a creature's happiness. Reason could only give a "weak and delusive guidance" and an "incompetent meddling" with the purpose of nature. The task would be much better done by the faculty of instinct because instinct does not require learning. Instinct does not act on the basis of prior experience. But reason requires both learning and experience, and thus inevitably leads to some bad choices. Therefore, instead of allowing reason to choose ends and the means to these ends, "nature would have trusted both to instinct alone."

If reason does not have the end or purpose of looking after a being's happiness, then it must have the only remaining function left for it and which only reason can accomplish, viz., producing a will which is good in itself and "good without regard to any further end" (397).

4.3 Good will and the concept of duty

The concept of duty includes that of good will. If we take up the challenge to think about the concept of duty, we need to think about how it is used in those cases in which it is true to say, "He acted solely from duty." Kant's method is to contrast "solely from duty" with such expressions as "contrary to duty" and "in accordance with duty." Here are five examples, only the last of which captures the essence of acting from duty.

4.3.1 Acts contrary to duty

Kant immediately rejects "acting contrary to duty" for the obvious reason that a person who lies, cheats or otherwise does the opposite of what duty commands could not be acting from duty. If it is wrong to lie, and I tell a lie, then I am not acting in accord with duty and therefore could not be acting from the duty not to lie.

4.3.2 Acts in accord with duty

But suppose that although I am given the opportunity to tell a lie ("Did you take the last cookie that was in the cookie jar?"), I tell the truth ("Yes, I took the last cookie."). In that case, I am acting in accord with duty. However, we do not yet know what motivated me to tell the truth, that is we do not know if I acted from duty.

4.3.3 Acts done from some selfish purpose

For example, I might have told the truth about taking the last cookie because I wanted to preserve a good reputation with the owner of the cookies and with others who might later hear from her that I am a person who can be trusted to tell the truth. In this case, although I acted in accord with the duty to tell the truth, I did not act from a duty (motive) to tell the truth. As Kant puts it, I am telling the truth because this "serves a selfish purpose." (397).

4.3.4 Acts done from immediate inclination

A more difficult case is one in which a person has an "immediate inclination" to do what is required by duty. Kant's reference is to persons who are so sympathetically constituted that... they find an inner pleasure in spreading joy around them...." They also get inner pleasure in relieving the suffering of others. Imagine a child of three or four years who is locked alone in a car, with windows shut, on a hot summer day. People who see this child will either immediately call the police or they will attempt to break the windows and pull the child out of the car. They may or may know that they have a duty of beneficence, but they do not act from duty. If they see that someone is suffering, they react to the child' suffering and will attempt to relieve it, not because they are thinking about what duty demands of them, but because they cannot bear to stand by when a child's life is at risk.

4.3.5 Acts done from duty

What Kant is looking for is a pure case of acting from duty, a case in which a person has no other motive than doing what moral principles command. Kant's example is a man who is so severely depressed that...

> *...all sympathy with the lot of others is extinguished, and suppose him still to have the power to benefit others in distress, even though he is not touched by their trouble because he is sufficiently absorbed with his own, and now suppose that, even though no inclination moves him any longer, he nevertheless tears himself from this deadly insensibility and performs the action without any inclination at all, but solely from duty (398).*

This is the case that Kant has been looking for and upon which he wants to lay the honorific title of an action that has genuine moral worth. It is a worth that is "far higher" than that of a "good-natured temperament" because "it is here that the worth of the character comes out." We might enjoy being around people who are good-natured but being good-natured gives them no moral credit or praise. It is much more difficult to be in the company of someone who is severely depressed, but who despite her own sorrows, does what duty demands. This, and only this is direct evidence of her moral character. She is a person of genuine moral worth.

4.4 Propositions of morality

Kant cites three propositions of morality, which presumably follow from the preceding analysis of the concept of a good will (Alison II, 5).

The first proposition, which is unstated but is implicit in the preceding examples, says that "an action must be done from duty in order to have any moral worth" (Ellington 12, fn. 12). This is illustrated by the example in the preceding section (4.3.5).

The second proposition says that "an action done from moral duty has its moral worth not in the purpose that is to be attained by it, but in the maxim according to which the action is determined" (399). As explained in the Introduction, a maxim is the subjective rule under which you act or intend to act. The moral worth of an action done from moral duty will be determined by the maxim alone, not by any incentives or effects of the action. These can only give to it a conditioned worth.

The third proposition, which Kant says follows from the other two, is expressed thus: "Duty is the necessity of an action done out of respect for the law" (400). If the act qualifies as an act done from duty, then it must be done out of respect for the law, that is, out of respect for the objective maxim or rule that applies universally, to all persons.

4.5 The categorical imperative

From these three propositions stated above, Kant draws the conclusion that "the pre-imminent good which is called moral can consist in nothing but the representation of the law in itself" (401). I must act only from the law itself if I am to act from duty and if I am to have genuine moral worth. What law should I act on that is consistent with a good will? Kant puts it this way:

> *"But what sort of law can be thought of which must determine the will without reference to any expected effect, so that the will can be absolutely good without qualification?"* (402).

If there is no purpose, instinct or inclination to which we can refer to explain this purity of will, then there is nothing left except "the universal conformity of [the will's] actions to law as such," that is, its conformity to the categorical imperative:

> *Act only according to that maxim whereby you can at the same time will that it should become a universal law* (402).

Kant draws a contrast between "being truthful from duty" and "being truthful from fear of disadvantageous consequences." In the first case the concept of an action itself contains a law for me, while in the second I must first look around elsewhere to see what the results for me are those that might be connected with the action.

> *For to deviate from the principle of duty is quite certainly bad; but to abandon my maxim of prudence can often be very advantageous for me, though to abide by it is certainly safer (403).*

Here is an example. Suppose that two white university students, returning drunk from an off-campus party, paint racist graffiti on the door of the dormitory room of an African American student. They are later asked by the campus police whether they painted the graffiti.

They are told that if they confess, then the punishment for painting the graffiti will be considerably less severe than it will be if they lie and are later found out to be the culprits (they will be suspended for one term, but not expelled from the university). Both students admit to painting the graffiti, but the first does so from the motive of duty (to always tell the truth), while the second tells the truth only because she does not want to risk the heavier sentence (expulsion). She tells the truth because she believes it is "safer" to abide by her maxim of prudence, although she has often found it advantageous to abandon her maxim when she deems it to be her advantage to do so.

This is where Kant would ask the game-changing question: "Would you really be content if your maxim of prudence (telling the truth only when it is to your advantage to do so) were to hold as a universal law for yourself as well as for others? Could you really say to yourself that everyone may lie when they find themselves in a difficulty from which she can find no other way to extricate herself?"

As previously noted in Chapter 2, Kant says of false (lying) promises (423), that one can "will a lie but cannot at all will a universal law to lie." In the student example, the lie is not about keeping a promise but about whether one has committed a wrongful act. It is a lie about what one has done in the past, not about what one will do in the future. Willing a universal law to lie about committing a wrongful act (if this is advantageous) would be "in vain" because no one would believe what I professed, "or if they over-hastily did believe, then they would pay me back in like coin" (that is, they would do the same to me). Therefore, my maxim of prudence "would necessarily destroy itself just as soon as it was made a universal law."

From examples like this we can discern what it is necessary for us to do to make our will morally good.

> *I only ask myself whether I can also will that my maxim should become a universal law. If not, then the maxim must be rejected, not because of any disadvantage accruing to me or even to*

others, but because it cannot be fitting as a principle in a possible legislation of universal law (403).

Kant adds to this that "reason exacts from me immediate respect for such legislation." He writes that "respect is an estimation of a worth that far outweighs any worth of what is recommended by inclination." When we act from the motive of duty (the condition of a good will), we are acting from pure respect for the practical law and from no other motive.

4.6 Philosophy as protector of the laws of duty

Kant concludes this section of *Grounding* by telling his readers that we have arrived at the principle of ordinary human reason by finding it a priori within the moral cognition of ordinary human reason. Kant is not claiming that ordinary reason thinks of this principle "abstractly in its universal form" (that is, as the categorical imperative). But "it does have it actually in view and does use it as the standard of judgment" (403-404). The proof of this is that ordinary reason "with this compass" in hand can easily distinguish between good and evil "in accord with duty, or contrary to duty." Neither science nor philosophy is needed for one to know "what one must do to be honest and good and even wise and virtuous."

What help can philosophy provide if we already know what is and what is not morally obligatory? Kant answers by reminding us that there is a constant struggle between what we know to be the commands of duty, as presented to us by reason, and our needs and inclinations "whose total satisfaction is summed up under the name of happiness" (405). Reason commands its precepts (for example, "Thou shalt always tell the truth") without promising to satisfy any inclination or need that will make us happy. This struggle makes us begin to question the validity of the strict laws of duty, "or at least upon their purity and strictness, and to make them, where possible, more compatible with our wishes and inclinations." The result is corruption of the laws of duty "in their very foundations and their whole dignity is destroyed—something which even ordinary practical reason cannot in the end call good" (405).

This is where philosophy can be useful. Philosophy can provide the "information and clear instruction" regarding the source of reason's own principle and how it differs from maxims based on need and inclination. In taking on this task, philosophy helps ordinary practical reason to "cultivate itself," thereby avoiding the risk of "losing all genuine moral principles through the ambiguity into which it easily falls." As Kant puts it, "peace will be found only in a thorough critical examination of our reason."

It is by such a critical examination (in the next chapter) that Kant will help cultivate practical reason by showing it how to avoid the corruption of its principle, the Categorical Imperative.

4.7 Questions for thought and discussion

1. What does Kant mean by "good without qualification"? In the following list, what things can be regarded as good without qualification? Wit, perseverance, honor, pleasure, happiness, self-control, a good will. Explain your answer.

2. One of the criticisms of the hedonist idea that happiness or pleasure is the ultimate good is that the source of the pleasure is irrelevant to determining its goodness. Thus, the pleasure of an assassin is equivalent to the pleasure of a person who spends her days feeding and caring for homeless children. How would Kant respond to this objection?

3. What makes a good will good?

4. Some critics of Kant complain about his declaration that a person who acts from a natural inclination to do good is not worthy of moral praise. For example, if you visit your elderly aunt in the hospital because you genuinely want to see her and make her feel better,

why would this not be at least as morally praiseworthy as visiting her from the sole motive of duty?

5. How do the propositions of morality (4.4) follow from the concept of a good will?

5. FROM POPULAR PHILOSOPHY TO METAPHYSICS

[*Grounding*, Second Section: Transition from Popular Moral Philosophy to a Metaphysics of Morals]

Kant earlier pronounced that his method is to "proceed analytically from ordinary knowledge to a determination of the supreme principle." He means that it was by a process of deduction from the idea of a good will and the concept of duty that he arrived at the categorical imperative. He accomplished this in the First Section.

The next step is to go "back again synthetically from an examination of this principle and its sources to ordinary knowledge where its application is found." Kant will exhibit several cases or possible real-life (ordinary) examples in which the categorical imperative might be used.

The first part of the synthetic examination takes place in the Second Section in which he proposes to "advance by natural stages" from "popular philosophy to metaphysics" (412). By "metaphysics," Kant means "pure rational knowledge separated from everything empirical" (409).

5.1 The concept of duty is not a concept of experience

In the First Section of *Grounding*, we have seen how Kant "drew out" the concept of duty from "the ordinary use of practical reason" (2.4.2.3). By a careful examination of how we use reason to decide what we morally ought to do, Kant analytically deduced (inferred) the concept of duty.

But what Kant discovered about this concept did not derive from experience. For example, there is no empirical evidence that an act done *in accord with* duty is also done *from* duty. You jump in the pool to save the child from drowning, but this does not tell us whether you did this from duty. It is possible that you acted out of self-love or from animal instinct. In fact, "there are always doubts as to whether what occurs has really been done from duty and so has moral worth" (406).

Kant goes further to assert that there is "absolutely no possibility by means of experience to make out with complete certainty a single case" in which an act that accords with duty has been done from duty (407). This is confusing because Kant earlier presented the example of the depressed man who gave help to others in distress even though he was not "touched" by their distress and had no inclination to help them. He did it only because he believed the moral law demanded that he give help to persons in need.

But even in this case, Kant says, "we can never, even by the strictest examination, completely plumb the depths of the secret incentives of our actions" (407). The point that Kant is trying to make is that even if we can never find (by empirical means) an actual case in which a person has acted only from duty, this is irrelevant. Kant's question is not whether there has ever been a situation in which a person has acted from duty, but what reason commands that a person ought to do.

Kant illustrates this with a helpful analogy. We all know what it is to be a sincere friend and we also know that "pure sincerity in friendship is required of every man." But we know this, "even though there might never yet have been a sincere friend" (408). This knowledge is not gained from experience. It is a priori knowledge of a duty "contained in the idea of a reason that determined the will..." (408). By analogy, we may never know whether we or anyone else has ever acted from the duty of beneficence, but we know a priori what reason commands us to do.

5.2 The moral law holds for all rational beings

The point was made earlier (3.2) that moral laws "are given a priori to humans as rational beings, not merely as human beings" (389). Moral laws must have their source "completely a priori in pure, but practical reason" (408). This cannot be achieved if the laws apply only to human beings. Being human is a contingent condition that makes moral laws merely empirical because they would be derived from such experiences as happiness and unhappiness, pleasure and pain and other human sensibilities. This would make it impossible for such laws to apply to all rational beings.

5.3 Morality cannot be derived from examples

I had earlier cited John Stuart Mill's distinction between the intuitive and the inductive school of ethics. The intuitive school holds that the principles of morals are "evident a priori," whereas the inductive school holds that "right and wrong… are questions of observation and experience." (3.4)

In this section of *Grounding*, Kant is clearly rejecting the inductive school's approach when he writes that "worse service cannot be rendered to morality than that an attempt be made to derive it from examples." The inductivist takes her examples of what is morally right and wrong from experience. But her examples would not have been judged "according to the principles of morality." Hence, we would have no way to determine whether they would be "fit" to serve as models (408).

Plato's Forms (ideas, concepts) are known intuitively, not inductively. We know what Triangularity, Beauty and Justice

are, not from our experience of triangular shapes, beautiful statues and just actions, but by our knowledge of the Form itself, what it essentially is. None of the triangles that we experience are a perfect representation of Triangularity because what we experience necessarily will have non-essential properties, for example, color and matter (think of a triangular flag). Hence, our knowledge of Triangularity and all forms could not have derived from experience. They must be known intuitively, that is, a priori (*Republic*, Book III 403-403, V 472-483, VI-VII 500-517 and several other dialogues).

If we would have no way of identifying a triangle that we see on the chalkboard as a triangle unless we had some grasp of the Form Triangularity, so Kant is arguing that we would have no way of knowing that an example we are given of a right action is a right action unless we have a standard to judge it as such. The standard is only to be found in the principles of morality. These principles are "the true original which lies in reason" (409) and can only be known a priori.

5.4 Advancing from popular philosophy to metaphysics

"Everything in nature works according to laws. Only a rational being has the power to act according to his conception of laws, i.e., according to principles, and thereby he has a will. Since reason is required for the derivation of actions from laws, the will is nothing other than practical reason." (412).

In the preface to *Grounding,* Kant made a distinction between laws of freedom (ethics) and laws of nature (physics). This is identical to the distinction between prescriptive and descriptive laws. The former is found in moral and political law and the latter are illustrative of the laws of science. A moral or legal rule prescribes human actions, for example, the rules prohibiting murder or requiring payment of taxes, but these rules can be disobeyed. The laws of science are descriptive, for example, laws describing planetary orbits. The planets are not required (prescribed) to keep to their orbiting paths. The laws of nature also apply to human behavior since that behavior is often beyond human control, for example, blushing, laughing or dreaming. We do not blush because we are morally required to blush. We blush because of physical causes that we cannot control.

The laws to which Kant refers in the preceding quote (412) are objective. This means that they are valid for every rational being as such (413). They are contrasted with maxims or subjective principles, which are valid only for the agent who adopts them. Because they are valid for every rational being, these principles apply to a perfectly rational as well as to finite, imperfectly rational agents, like you or me (Allison III,6).

If a rational being has the power to act according to prescriptive laws (subjective or objective), "thereby he has a will." If it is reason that determines the will, then the will can choose that which reason dictates, "independent of inclination." For example, it may be your inclination to keep the wallet you have just found on the sidewalk, but reason dictates that you make a serious effort to find the owner of the wallet. What you choose to do depends on the nature of your will.

If reason "infallibly determines the will," then actions which are recognized as being objectively necessary are also subjectively necessary. If reason does not determine the will, and it "submits also to subjective conditions" (e.g. the desire to keep the wallet you found), then one's actions are "subjectively contingent." Kant fully recognizes the real possibility that the will of a rational being may not necessarily follow objective principles of reason "because of its own nature."

5.5 Imperatives

When an objective principle necessitates the will it is called a command of reason, "and the formula of the command is called an imperative" (413). "Imperatives say that something would be good to do or to refrain from doing," but they say it to a will that does not always do it, simply because it has been represented to it as something that it is good to do.

> *Consequently, imperatives are only formulas for expressing the relation of objective laws of willing in general to the subjective interpretation of the will of this or that rational being, e.g., the human will* (414).

For example, the imperative "Do not lie" provides the instruction (formula) not to lie, but this is subject to our freedom to do or not to do what we believe the imperative commands.

5.5.1 Hypothetical and categorical imperatives

If you stop your car for pedestrians in a crosswalk because you are afraid that you might get caught and fined, you might be acting on the imperative "Obey traffic laws when it suits your purposes." But if you stop for pedestrians in a crosswalk because you believe you have a moral obligation to obey the traffic laws, then you might be acting on the imperative "Obey all laws because they are laws." The former is called a hypothetical imperative – it represents an action as a means for attaining something else that one wants. The latter is called a categorical imperative – it represents an action as "objectively necessary in itself, without reference to another end."

This is the generic use of "categorical imperative." It refers to a class of imperatives, not to the supreme principle (CI). When Kant writes about ordinary moral rules, e.g. "Thou shall not lie," he refers to them as categorical imperatives because they command behavior categorically. The supreme principle also commands categorically but since it is supreme, we will refer to it with capital letters: Categorical Imperative (or just CI).

Many other examples of hypothetical imperatives come to mind. They are most familiar when we give prudential advice, for example, "You should enroll at a California state university if you want a good undergraduate education" or "You ought to take the Amtrak Coast Starlight if you want a beautiful train ride". The form of these expression is conditional: "You ought to do X if you want Y." If Y is not desired, then X becomes irrelevant.

General imperatives of skill are hypothetical, that is, they tell us whether the action is good for some purpose. Whether or not they give good advice depends entirely on the purpose.

> *The prescriptions needed by a doctor in order to make his patient thoroughly healthy and by a poisoner in order to make sure of killing his victim are of equal value so far as each serve to bring about its purpose perfectly"* (415).

A person who admits that she tells the truth and keeps her promises only because she wants to maintain a good reputation in her community represents her imperative as hypothetical. She conceives of telling the truth and keeping promises as means to an end, not as actions that are objectively necessary. She tells the truth because she believes that not telling the truth might result in the loss of a job and the loss of friends. She teaches her young children not to steal because "you might get caught," not because "it is the wrong thing to do."

The lesson Kant wants us to learn from these examples is that a hypothetical imperative does not qualify as a moral rule. If you tell your child not to lie, you are giving her practical advice about how to stay out of trouble. If you want to give your child moral advice, then you should tell her to tell the truth, but without a condition attached. A moral lesson is about duty. It is not a lesson about how not to get caught, how to maintain a good reputation with others, how not to avoid punishment, and generally, how not to avoid bad consequences.

The distinction between hypothetical and categorical imperatives was noticed by Plato twenty-four hundred years ago, although he did not use Kant's terminology. In *Republic,* Plato had the character Glaucon distinguish between a "completely just" and a "completely unjust" person. The former person will pursue justice for its own sake, not because this pursuit will lead to good consequences. Indeed, the just person will continue to be just even if he has a false reputation for being completely unjust. The challenge for Socrates in the dialogue is to show that although justice is good for its consequences, it is also good for itself, as something to be desired for its own sake (357b). Although "good for itself" did not mean the same thing for Plato as it meant for Kant, the attempt to justify moral behavior as commanded categorically is a common goal for both philosophers.

Categorical imperatives command absolutely. They defer to no purpose (end). "They declare an action to be objectively necessary without reference to any end." Second, the imperative is "not concerned with the matter of the action but with its form and the principle from which it follows; what is essentially good in the action consists in the mental disposition, let the consequences be what they may." Kant calls this the imperative "of morality." (416). For example, "I ought not to lie even though lying were to bring me not the slightest discredit" (441). And, Kant would add, even if lying had good consequences for others, I ought always to tell the truth.

In an essay that appeared in 1799, Kant defended the position that telling the truth is an absolute duty, admitting of no exceptions. According to his critic, Kant would have us say that "it would be a crime to tell a lie to a murderer who asked us whether our friend who is being pursued by the murderer had taken ref-

uge in our house". **Kant agrees that this is exactly what he would say because truthfulness is "an unconditional duty which holds in all circumstances" If a consequence of telling the truth is that the man who had taken refuge is found and killed by the murderer, Kant would agree that this is a bad consequence, but consequences have nothing to do with determinations of one's duty (Kant, *On a Supposed Right to Lie*).**

5.5.2 The concept of a categorical imperative

Kant asks us to compare the concept of a categorical imperative with the concept of a hypothetical imperative. The main distinction between them is that in the latter case, "I do not know beforehand what it will contain until its condition is given." Since a hypothetical imperative says, "You ought to do X if you want Y," we do not know what we ought to do (X) until we find out the condition (Y). Thus, I won't know that I ought to change the tire until I find out that the tire is flat (punctured, losing air, sidewall damaged, etc.).

But in the case of a categorical imperative, "I know immediately what it contains." It says categorically "You ought to do X." There are no conditions attached to the imperative. It commands absolutely and universally. And it is a maxim that must conform "to the universality of the law as such."

Hence, there is only one categorical imperative and it is this:

> *Act only according to that maxim whereby you can at the same time will that it should become a universal law.*

All imperatives of duty can be derived from this one imperative as their principle. This is the supreme principle we discussed in the Introduction: The Categorical Imperative (CI). Since there are several versions of CI (to be discussed below), scholars usually refer to this version as the Formula of Universal Law (UL).

5.5.3 Duties derived from the formula of universal law

Kant divides his examples into *duties to ourselves* and *duties to others*. He then divides each of these into *perfect* and *imperfect duties*.

Kant writes in a footnote that a perfect duty is a duty "which permits no exception in the interest of inclination" (422, fn. 12). He means that it is a duty not to do an action even if I want to do it – I have no choice. For example, the duty not to kill, assault, rape, or destroy the property of others applies to all persons, not to a few select persons of my choosing. Imperfect duties, however, permit exceptions in the interest of inclination – I have a choice. For example, the duty to help others gives me the choice of whom to help, how many to help, and when to help.

Kant mentions in the same footnote that this division of duties is arbitrary (421, fn. 12). He realizes that there are other ways of dividing perfect and imperfect duties. For example, some philosophers divide duties by their relationship to rights. A perfect duty not to harm another is reciprocal with a right of all others not to be harmed by anyone at any time. An imperfect duty to help another person who is in need is not reciprocal with a right to be helped.

In *Grounding*, Kant discusses two examples of duties to oneself: the perfect duty not to commit suicide and the imperfect duty to develop one's natural talents. He also discusses two examples of duties to others: the perfect duty not to make a lying promise and the imperfect duty to benefit others. The example of the perfect duty to others was previously discussed in the Introduction. Here are Kant's accounts of the remaining examples:

5.5.3.1 The perfect duty (to oneself) not to commit suicide

Kant's example of a perfect duty to oneself is about a man who is...

> *...reduced to despair by a series of misfortunes [who] feels sick of life but is still so far in possession of his reason that he can ask himself whether taking his own life would not be contrary to his duty to himself" (422).*

Recall the two steps suggested by Kant when answering this question for this unfortunate man. First, he must formulate a subjective maxim: "From self-love I make as my principle to shorten my life when its continued duration threatens more evil than it promises satisfaction." Second, he must ask whether this principle of self-love can become a universal law of nature.

> *One sees at once a contradiction in a system of nature whose law would destroy life by means of the very same feeling that acts so as to stimulate the furtherance of life, and hence there could be no existence as a system of nature. Therefore, such a maxim cannot possibly hold as a universal law of nature and is, consequently, wholly opposed to the supreme principle of duty (422).*

By "a contradiction" Kant means that it is a logical impossibility for there to be a universal law that morally permits one to commit suicide whenever he believes that his life is intolerable. This law is impossible because there is a competing strong feeling or instinct that causes people to do whatever is necessary to preserve their own life. Hence, a universal law permitting suicide "can have no existence" in this system of nature.

It is difficult for some to accept Kant's argument that it is a duty to oneself to remain alive that makes suicide morally wrong. We all recognize those cases in which a person wants to commit suicide but refrains for religious reasons. For example, she believes that God is her creator and as such He "owns" her body. Her duty is to God not to herself. She remains alive because she believes that only God has the right to destroy her. There are others who are suicidal but resist killing themselves because they have duties to others, for example, they have young children or other loved ones who would be hurt by their demise. Her duty is to her loved ones, not to herself.

5.5.3.2 The imperfect duty to oneself to cultivate one's talents

Kant asks us to imagine a man who "finds in himself a talent whose cultivation could make him a man useful in many respects. But he finds himself in comfortable circumstances and prefers to indulge in pleasure rather than to bother himself about broadening and improving his fortunate natural aptitudes" (423).

Let us further suppose that this man wants to know whether he has a duty to others to cultivate these talents. The maxim he proposes to act under is "I will ignore my natural gifts and indulge in a life of pleasure, if this is my inclination."

Kant notes that this maxim could be adopted as a universal law, that is, it is possible that all persons could let their talents rust while devoting their lives "entirely to idleness, indulgence, propagation and, in a word, to enjoyment" (423). We can imagine a society in which no one does what they have a natural talent to do, but instead does whatever they enjoy doing. A woman with a natural gift for music instead decides to train as an airplane mechanic, and a man with a natural talent for mathematics decides to ignore this natural gift and live a life emulating the late Hugh Hefner.

But he cannot possibly will that this should become a universal law of nature or be implanted in us as such a law by a natural instinct. For as a rational being he necessarily wills that all his faculties be developed, inasmuch as they are given him for all sorts of possible purposes (423).

It is in the concept of a rational being that Kant finds the contradiction. Being rational implies willing the development of all of one's faculties. It defies rationality to will a universal law that allows us to ignore our natural gifts. In other words, we cannot both will the development of our faculties and at the same time universalize a maxim that makes it morally permissible to not will the development of our faculties.

5.5.3.3 The imperfect duty to benefit others

Duties to benefit others can also be called duties of charity. Kant's example is of a man "who finds things going well for himself but sees others (whom he could help) struggling with great hardships, and he thinks 'What does it matter to me?'"

But the same man has enough conscience to have the maxim upon which he is acting put to the test of UL. His maxim is: "If I have no desire to help others in need, then I shall not help them, even when I have sufficient resources to give help."

Can this this man will this maxim to become a universal law? Here is Kant's reply:

...even though it is possible that a universal law of nature could subsist in accordance with that maxim, still it is impossible to will that such a principle should hold everywhere as a law of nature. For a will which resolved in this way would contradict itself, inasmuch as cases might often arise in which one should have need of the love and sympathy of others and in which he would deprive himself, by such a law of nature springing from his own will, of all hope of the aid he wants for himself (423).

We can imagine a society in which no one gives help to those in need, but we cannot imagine consciously willing that everyone adopt and act on the maxim that we do not have a duty to give charitable help to those in need. If we urged the universal adoption of this maxim we would be "depriving ourselves" of receiving the help of others in those situations in which we might find ourselves in need of their help. Hence, "a will which resolved in this way would contradict itself."

There is a distinction between a contradiction in thinking and a contradiction in willing that is parallel to the distinction between perfect and imperfect duties. Hence, not making a lying promise is a contradiction in thinking because it is logically impossible to universalize the maxim to make lying promises whenever you wish. By way of contrast, the maxim "I shall never help others in need," can be universalized without logical contradiction. But there would still be "a contradiction in willing" because one would presumably not want to have her subjective maxim universalized because of the possibility that someday she might find herself needing the help of others (with thanks to Paul Miklowitz for suggesting this parallel distinction).

5.5.4 The second formulation of CI: the end in itself

As mentioned earlier, Kant gives several different formulations (versions) of CI. It is important to understand that these are versions of the same principle, not different principles. Remember that the first formulation (at 2.5.1) is The Formula of Universal Law (UL).

A second formulation, perhaps more popular and frequently quoted in scholarly articles and textbooks on ethical theory is The Formula of the End in Itself (EI). It says:

Act in such a way that you treat humanity, whether in your own person or in the person of another, always at the same time as an end and never simply as a means (429).

Although EI appears to be quite different than UL, Kant claims that they have the same essential components. In order to understand how this is so, we must look backwards again to see how Kant arrived at EI.

Professor Henry Allison provides a helpful line of argument that underlies Kant's claim that the categorical imperative presupposes an end (Allison III, 8). It runs as follows:

1.   Since ends are the sources of reasons to act, if an agent has no end in view, then that agent would have no reason to act.

2.   But any imperative presupposes that there are reasons to act and a categorical imperative presupposes that these reasons are valid for all rational agents, which entails that they must be independent of any interests that are not shared by every conceivable rational agent.

3.   This entails that there must be an end that is likewise independent of any such interests; otherwise it would not be universally valid.

4.   Such an end, by definition, would be an end in itself.

5.   Therefore, if there is a categorical imperative, there must be something that exists as an end in itself.

Allison also points out that (according to Kant) any end capable of grounding a categorical imperative must meet two distinct conditions: (a) it must be objective, that is, given by pure reason and be valid for all rational agents, regardless of their inclinations.; and (b) it must be self-standing, that is, it must be a source of reasons to act or to refrain from acting. Presumably, both conditions are met in what Kant describes as "something whose existence in itself [has] an absolute worth."

A human being (as a rational being) meets conditions (a) and (b), and therefore qualifies as an end capable of grounding a categorical imperative.

> *Now I say that the human being and in general every rational being exists as an end in itself, not merely as means for the discretionary use of this or that will, but must in all his actions, whether directed to himself or also to other rational beings, always be regarded at the same time as an end (428)*

And this gives us EI:

> *"Act in such a way that you treat humanity, whether in your own person or in the person of another, always at the same time as an end and never simply as a means."*

It has been said that because "we are all too often inclined not to respect persons, not to value them as they ought to be valued," that Kant emphasizes EI as an important formulation of the categorical imperative.

Central to Kant's ethical theory is the claim that all persons are owed respect just because they are persons, that is, free rational beings. To be a person is to have a status and worth that is unlike that of any other kind of being: it is to be an end in itself with dignity. And the only response that is appropriate to such a being is respect. Respect (that is, moral recognition respect) is the acknowledgment in attitude and conduct of the dignity of persons as ends in themselves. Respect for such beings is not only appropriate but also morally and unconditionally required: the status and worth of persons is such that they must always be respected (R. Dillon).

Respect for persons is reciprocal with their dignity as ends in themselves. It is an important element of Kantian ethics that has historically set it apart from all other ethical theories.

5.5.5 Examples of duties derived from the formula of the end in itself

Kant turns to the same examples he used to show how duties are derived from UL (2.5.3). If EI is in fact only another version of CI, then the results should be identical to what was found when applying UL to the same cases.

5.5.5.1 The perfect duty (to oneself) not to commit suicide

If we agree with Kant's idea that we have duties to ourselves that are not also duties to others, then "the man who contemplates suicide will ask himself whether his action can be consistent with the idea of humanity as an end in itself" (429). Kant contends that any suicide that is done with the motive to "escape from a difficult situation," is a use of one's own person "as a means to maintain a tolerable condition till the end of his life."

This leaves one wondering whether a woman who is on the top floor of a burning building and decides to jump to her death instead of waiting to be consumed by the fire is escaping from a "difficult" situation that she should have "tolerated" until she burned to death.

5.5.5.2 The perfect duty to others not to make a lying promise

This case was first discussed in the Introduction. The question now is not whether the liar can universalize the maxim under which he acts, but whether the act of lying to another is to intend to make use of another person merely as a means to an end which the latter does not otherwise hold. This leads to the general question whether any lie to another is to use that person as a means to an end to which that person has not agreed.

The case of the promise to repay a loan at an agreed upon time while secretly not intending to repay it, seems to be an excellent case of using another to reach one's own ends without their consent. But what about so-called "white lies," in which you say that you have only that person's best interest in mind when you tell the lie. For example, a physician tells a woman the lie that she will soon go into remission and the cancer will disappear. Or a student who has just returned from a ski trip where she broke her leg, tells her mother by phone that

"Everything went well. I had a great time." In both cases, the reason for telling the lie is "I didn't want him/her to suffer by telling the truth."

It is obvious that Kant's new formula (EI) will not permit even a white lie. In both of the previous cases, the liar is manipulating what the person knows in order to achieve an end or purpose. The fact that the liar believes that his or her end is "noble," does not justify the lie any more than it would justify it if the end was ignoble.

In a footnote to this section Kant argues that the oft-cited Golden Rule "Do not do to others what you do not want done to yourself" does not qualify as a moral standard or principle. "It cannot be a universal law, for it contains the ground neither of duties to oneself nor of duties of love toward others" (430, fn 23). Kant gives the counter example of a man who would "gladly consent that others should not benefit him, if only he might be excused from benefitting them." Nor does the Golden Rule contain the ground of strict duties toward others. For example, we can imagine a criminal using the Golden Rule as a justification for being "able to dispute with the judges who punish him." If a judge accused of a crime would want the opportunity to dispute his punishment, then the judge should allow other criminals the same opportunity. Perhaps a better counterexample would be the person who does not care if others lie to him. He usually knows when someone is lying, and it is more important to this man that he "gets away" with telling lies to them whenever this is to his advantage. Thus, although he violates the universal law, he is not in violation of the Golden Rule.

5.5.5.3 The imperfect duty to oneself to cultivate one's talents

This duty is best explained with an example. Suppose you have greater talents at physics than Albert Einstein. But you decide that (like Einstein) you would also like to learn to play the violin and play it well. In this case, you can do both. Learning to play the violin does not conflict with "humanity in one's person as an end in itself." But it would conflict if you entirely disregarded your natural talents in physics to concentrate on becoming a great violinist.

Kant stipulates that "there are in humanity capacities for greater perfection which belong to the end that nature has in view as regards humanity in our own person" (430). If this is true (Kant offers no proof), then the neglect of these capacities "would not be consistent with this end." Thus, by taking up the violin and ignoring physics, you would have failed to treat your humanity as an end in itself.

5.5.5.4 The imperfect duty to benefit others

Kant points out that we clearly have a negative duty not to prevent others from achieving the natural end of their own happiness. But obedience to this duty does not further the happiness of others. We must also strive to "harmonize" our behavior with humanity as an end in itself.

For the ends of any subject who is an end in himself must as far as possible be my ends also, if that conception of an end in itself is to have its full effect in me. (430).

Professor Allison has doubts about Kant's argument for both imperfect duties. He rightly wonders how an essentially negative concept of an end in itself could yield positive duties (whether to oneself or others).

Kant attempts to clarify the situation by distinguishing between a negative and positive agreement with the requirement to treat human beings as ends in themselves, which was implicit in the previous example [of duties to oneself]. Presumably, the former consists in not treating human beings merely as means, while the latter requires fully respecting their status as ends in themselves. But even granting this distinction, it remains unclear why the latter should require going as far as making, to the extent possible, the ends of others one's own, as contrasted, say, with the occasional performance of acts of kindness (Allison III, 8, V).

For example, if I hire a jobless man to do some house painting, I want to make sure that I do not take advantage of his jobless status. So I tell him that I will pay him the same hourly fee that I would pay to a fully employed house painter, and I am careful to ask him if this is acceptable. If he accepts the job, then although I am using him as a means to get my house painted, I am also treating him as an end in himself by securing his agreement to a fair fee for his work. Now it may be true that this man has other ends, for example, he may want to secure a full-time job. Although I may be sympathetic with this end, I am under no positive obligation to give him a full-time job or find one for him. His ends need not always be my ends.

5.5.6 The third formulation of CI: autonomy of the will

The principle of autonomy of the will (AW) assumes that "the idea of the will of every rational being is a will that legislates universal law." The imperative is that we ought to

Act in such a way that as a member of a systematic union of rational beings, one legislates in universal laws while also being himself subject to these laws (431).

According to this principle all maxims are rejected which are not consistent with the will's own legislation of universal law. The will is thus not merely subject to the law but is subject to the law in such a way that it must be regarded also as legislating for itself and only on this account as being subject to the law (of which it can regard itself as the author)

In imperative form, Kant means that we ought to reject any maxim which we would not legislate for ourselves. This formula is a consequence of the combination of the formula of universal law (UL at 2.5.2) and the formula of an end in itself (EI at 2.5.5).

The ground of all practical legislation lies objectively in the rule and in the form of universality, which (according to the first principle) makes it capable of being a law (perhaps even a law of nature). Subjectively, however, it lies in the end; but the subject of all ends is every rational being as an end in itself (according to the second principle): from this now follows our third practical principle of the will, as the supreme condition of its agreement with universal practical reason, the idea of the will of every rational being as a will giving universal law. (431)

How does AW follow? First, AW clearly incorporates UL. If UL tells us to test each maxim by asking whether we can consistently will it to be adopted and acted upon by everyone, then this repeats the imperative of AW. But how does AW incorporate the second formulation (EI)? Kant's reply is that all practical legislation "subjectively...lies in the end." The end is either a rational being who sets the ends, or it is all rational beings who are the object of those ends, namely "the same rational beings qua end-setters" (Allison, III, 9, I). If it is the former (a rational being who sets the ends), then each rational being determines for themselves what maxims can become universal law. If it is the latter (a rational being who is the object of the ends), then we get the same result because all of those who are the objects of the legislation are also the end-setters.

Some have interpreted Kant's use of the word "subjective" as meaning that each person can create and impose upon himself any moral rule of his choosing. But this is not what Kant means by "subjective." He means that one has "no need for some non-moral incentive to obey the dictates of the law," (Allison, id.) for example, fear of the negative opinion of others. If any incentive is required, this undermines the categorical status of UL. In other words, if some non-moral interest must be presupposed in order to have an incentive to obey moral requirements, then the necessitation expressed in these requirements is conditional and the imperative is merely hypothetical.

In previous attempts of philosophers to discover the principle of morality, "duty was never discovered, but only the necessity of acting from a certain interest" (433). The interest sought was either the interest of oneself or the interest of others, for example, my own pleasure or the pleasure of others. "Either way the imperative had to be always conditional and could never serve as a command." The only option remaining for the discovery of duty is to begin with the premise that...

"Man is subject to his own, yet universal, legislation and that he is bound only to act in accordance with his own will, which is, however, a will purposed by nature to legislate universal law" (433, my emphasis).

The italicized words indicate clearly why Kant calls his principle "autonomy of the will."

These words mark a clear distinction between the formula of autonomy of the will from every other principle proposed in the history of philosophical ethics. Kant organizes all other principles under the word "heteronomy" (the antonym of "autonomy," meaning "under the subjection of others").

5.5.7 The fourth formulation of CI: the kingdom of ends

The fourth and last version of the categorical imperative "leads to another very fruitful concept," namely that of a kingdom of ends.

By "kingdom" I understand a systematic union of different rational beings through common laws... All rational beings stand under the law that each of them should treat himself and all others never merely as means but always at the same time as an end in himself. Hereby arises a systematic union of rational beings through common objective laws, i.e., a kingdom that may be called a kingdom of ends (certainly only an ideal), inasmuch as these laws have to view the very relation of such beings to one another as ends and means (433).

The imperative for every rational being that emerges from this is: "Act as if you are through your maxim always a legislating member in the universal kingdom of ends" (KE).

Kant explains that KE forces us to abstract from our personal differences and from the content of our private ends. This makes it possible to think of "a whole of all ends in systematic connection (a whole both of rational beings as ends in themselves and also of the particular ends which each may set for himself)" (433)   That is, one can think of a kingdom of ends that is possible on the aforesaid principles (UL, EI and AW).

Allison points out that in the next paragraph, Kant links KE specifically with EI, suggesting that a kingdom of ends could be brought about if everyone would treat themselves and others "never merely as means, but always at the same time as an end in itself" (III, 2, 9).

5.6 Comparing all formulas of the categorical imperative

Although we have described four versions or formulas of the categorical imperative, Kant writes that there are "three ways of representing the principle of morality" (436).   There is no conflict here. Kant means that there are three versions of The Formula of Universal Law (UL), namely the formulas of: End in Itself (EI), Autonomy of the Will (AW), and Kingdom of Ends (KE).

Kant writes that these ways of representing the principle of morality "are at bottom only so many formulas of the very same law: one of them by itself contains a combination of the other two" (436).   There has been a great deal of debate among Kant scholars about whether this claim is true (see references below), which I will not attempt to duplicate here.

However, instead of proving that any one formula is a combination of the other two, Kant says that all maxims have (1) a form, that is, "maxims must be so chosen as if they were to hold as universal laws of nature"; (2) a matter, that is, a rational being is an end in himself and thus "must serve in every maxim as a condition limiting all merely relative and arbitrary ends"; and (3) "A complete determination of all maxims by the formula that all maxims proceeding from his own legislation ought to harmonize with a possible kingdom of ends as a kingdom of nature" (436).

This means that any subjective maxim that satisfies (1), (2) and (3) ipso facto can be adopted as an objective maxim not only under UL, but also under EI, AW and KE. Thus, I can test the subjective maxim "I will never steal the property of another person," by asking whether it can be adopted as a universal law of nature, whether it treats rational being as ends in themselves, whether it is self-created, and if legislated, whether it will harmonize with the legislation of all rational beings. If the answer is uniformly affirmative, then this is enough to show that all versions "represent the same principle."

Kant's last word on this topic is about how to promulgate (advertise) the supreme moral principle. He writes that it would be better for us to use UL ("Act according to that maxim which can at the same time make itself a universal law") because of its "rigor." But if one wants to "secure acceptance" for the moral law, Kant's advice is "to bring one and the same action under the three aforementioned principles [EI, AW and KE] and thus, as far as possible, to bring the moral law nearer to intuition (he means "closer to feeling").

During my many years of teaching Kant to undergraduate students, I found that EI is not only more understandable but more intuitive and therefore more acceptable than the original formulation of the Categorical Imperative (UL).

5.7 Summary: from a good will to autonomy and back again

In the first paragraph at 437, Kant writes "We can now end where we started at the beginning, viz., the concept of an unconditionally good will." Kant here explains how this has happened, and in so doing he conveniently summarizes the entire rational process that ends with the categorical imperative, as it is formulated in the principle of autonomy of the will (AW).

We started with Kant's definition of an unconditionally good will as "a will that requires nothing to qualify it as good." Intelligence, pleasure, wisdom, and moderation must combine with a good will to qualify as good, but a good will does not require anything as a condition of its goodness. A good will can never be evil (2.1).

The maxim of a good will is to always act from duty. Although there is some controversy about this maxim (Wood §2), Kant's claim is that when we act from duty, we not only act in accord with the maxim that applies to our situation, but our sole motive is to do what the maxim commands (2.4.2.3). For example, you tell the truth not from the motive of obtaining the favor or avoiding the displeasure of others, but only from the pure motive of wanting to tell the truth, irrespective of any other existing inclination.

The only law that can be thought of which determines the will without reference to any expected effect, so that the will can be absolutely good without qualification is the categorical imperative (402). The imperative cannot be hypothetical (e.g. "Always tell the truth if you want to maintain a good reputation") for this would place a limiting condition on the will (i.e., the expected effect).

Second, when the good will chooses a maxim, it must be one that "when made into a universal law, can never conflict with itself." The only condition under which a will can never be in conflict with itself is the categorical imperative: "Act according to maxims which can at the same time have for their object themselves as universal laws of nature."

This brings us back to the formula for an absolutely good will. When you act on a maxim that has the universal law and nothing else as its object; for example, when you conceive of telling the truth as an absolute obligation with no connection to any other motive, then you display an "absolutely good will." And the circle is complete – we have now returned to where we started.

5.8 Autonomy and heteronomy

As noted above (5.7), autonomy of the will is "the property of the will being a law to itself (independently of any property of the objects of volition)." In the parenthetical clause Kant means that the will has the capacity to act or refrain from acting independently of any subject it might regard as good, e.g. pleasure, virtue, wisdom). It is as a property of the will that autonomy now serves as the supreme principle of morality.

This is a bit confusing. We began with CI as the supreme moral principle, only to learn that it was renamed as the Formula of Universal Law (UL). Kant has now given the honorific of supremacy to the Formula of Autonomy of the Will, while still maintaining that all formulas are no more than versions of the Categorical Imperative.

Heteronomy is characterized by Kant "as the source of all spurious principles of morality." The word "spurious" should alert us that heteronomy can never produce a categorical imperative, and that all moral principles not based on autonomy are forms of heteronomy.

In every case where an object of the will must be laid down as the foundation for prescribing a rule to determine the will, there the rule is nothing but heteronomy. The imperative is then conditioned, viz., if or because one wills this object (pleasure, health, well-being), one should act thus or so. Hence, the imperative can never command morally, i.e., categorically. But a categorical imperative says that "I ought to act this way or that way, even though I did not will something else."

The moral imperative must therefore abstract from every object to such an extent that no object has any influence at all on the will, so that practical reason (the will) may not merely minister to an interest not belonging to it but may merely show its own commanding authority as the supreme legislation.

We will return to Kant's objections to heteronomous principles when we compare Kant's moral theory to the theories of Plato, John Locke and John Stuart Mill in Chapter 9.

5.9 Questions for thought and discussion

1. Why does Kant claim that "the concept of duty is not a concept of experience"?

2. Examples of ethical decision-making are very important for purposes of clarification in philosophical ethics. Why, then does Kant contend that "worse service cannot be rendered morality than that an attempt be made to derive it from examples"?

3. What is the difference between hypothetical and categorical imperatives? Give two examples of your own to illustrate the distinction.

4. Can moral imperatives ever be hypothetical? Explain.

5. Critique Kant's example of an imperfect duty to oneself not to commit suicide. Is the universalization of a subjective rule not to commit suicide a logical contradiction?

6. Is there a perfect duty not to commit pedophilia? Sexual harassment? Cruelty to animals? Explain.

7. Discuss the end-in-itself (EI) formulation of the categorical imperative. Does it successfully show that one has a duty to maximize one's natural talents? Explain.

8. Is the Golden Rule in conformity with the end-in-itself formulation of the categorical imperative?

9. The principle of autonomy of the will (AW) is "the idea of the will of every rational being as a will that legislates universal law."

This seems to imply that whatever rule I want to govern my life is a rule that everyone else should adopt. Kant goes even farther than this by suggesting that it is only because duties are self-imposed that they can be unconditionally binding. Explain.

10. The final version of the categorical imperative is the formula of the kingdom of ends (KE). What does this formula say that is not already said in the preceding formulas? How can it be used to decide whether a moral rule should be universally adopted?

6 A FREE WILL AND A WILL UNDER MORAL LAW

[*Grounding*, Third Section: Transition from a Metaphysics of Morals to a Critique of Pure Practical Reason]

This chapter is optional. Most introductory courses in philosophy do not include a commentary on the Third Section of Grounding. This is partly because Kant has already finished the task he set for himself in the Preface, namely: "seeking out and establishing the supreme principle of morality" (392). The second reason is that the Third Section is denser than the material in the first and second sections (chapters 3 -5). James Ellington, the translator of the Hackett edition of *Grounding* cautioned readers (in a footnote) that the Third Section is "difficult to grasp" (445, fn 31).

However, for those who wish to "soldier on" to the end of Grounding, here is a brief account and analysis. One reward for continuing is that Kant gives a unique defense of freedom of the will and a strong rejection of philosophical determinism.

If Kant has established the supreme moral principle, why does he assert that there is more to do? Kant's first reply is that he has not yet provided a justification (deduction) of the categorical imperative. This may come as a surprise because we have been led to believe that the categorical imperative was previously deduced in stages from the concept of a good will.

What Kant means is that he has not yet deduced the categorical imperative from both the moral law and "the presupposition of freedom." (Allison, IV, 3: 10). If rational beings are not free to make moral choices, then there is no point in giving them a supreme moral principle to guide their choices.

In the first of three parts of the Third Section, while in the process of attempting to provide a deduction (justification) of the categorical imperative, Kant makes the claim that "a free will and a will under moral laws are one and the same thing." Kant scholars refers to this as the "reciprocity thesis." In defending this thesis, Kant proves that having a free will is both a necessary and a sufficient condition for being under the moral law. That is, if we are beings who are under the moral law, we have freedom of the will and if we have a free will, then ipso facto we are beings who are under the moral law.

That we must have freedom of the will in order to be under the moral law is relatively easy to prove. To be "under" the moral law is to have the capacity to understand that the law applies to our conduct and the law also provides a reason for one's behavior. To be under the moral law is not like being under physical law. If you sit on a broken chair and it collapses beneath you, then the law of gravity applies to what has happened to you, and you would refer to the law of gravity as an explanation of your fall. But if you are thinking about cheating on an important examination, then the law prohibiting deception applies to what you intentionally do, and you would refer to the moral law as a reason for your decision not to cheat. If you have a moral reason for deciding how to behave, then there is a presumption of freedom, namely that you could have done otherwise. If you have an explanation for something that happened to you (falling from a broken chair), there is no presumption of freedom – you could not have helped it.

Having a free will is also a sufficient condition for being under the moral law. If rational beings endowed with a will are faced with a choice between alternative courses of action, then there must be a moral law that serves as a guide for them (448). Morality can only be derived from the property of freedom. "Freedom belongs universally to the activity of rational beings endowed with a will"

In philosophy, determinism is the theory that all events, including moral choices, are completely determined by previously existing causes. Determinism is opposed to the doctrine of free will because the latter entails that human choices are uncaused. Kant's response is that if there is no free will, then morality is impossible in the sense that blame could never attach to an otherwise immoral act. If one could not do otherwise than to lie, cheat or steal, then no one could be held responsible for such behavior. If no one is responsible for what they do, then a moral law telling us what we ought to do is pointless. The challenge for Kant is to show that it is plausible to think that humans are free, despite the fact that natural, or causal, determinism exists in the empirical world.

Kant makes a distinction between humans as rational beings and humans as empirical beings. As empirical beings human behavior is subject to physical law, for example, the law of gravity. As rational beings humans are self-determining, that is, they are subject to their own laws and they make their own moral choices. "We must attribute to every being endowed with reason and a will this property of determining itself to action under the idea of its own freedom" (449).

It follows that the doctrine of determinism is not relevant as an account of the moral choices of rational beings. Determinism applies only to physical events in nature, not to our use of reason. The idea that every event has a cause applies to physical change, including changes in the human body ("His heart attack was caused by a blocked coronary artery"). It does not apply at all to a will determined by reason, including moral decisions ("Her decision to help the poor was based on the belief that this was her duty").

Why is this? Let's begin to answer this by making a distinction between two kinds of determinism (causality): *physical determinism*, as in "Billiard ball A hit billiard ball B, causing B to roll into the pocket" and *rational determinism*, as in "If A is B and B is C, then A is C." Rational determinism is no more than logical implication: the premises determine or cause the conclusion. When Kant uses the word "reason" he means the faculty by which we make logical inferences from given premises or from determinate objects (concepts). We can think of the premises or concepts as determining a conclusion in the sense that the conclusion is contained in the premises or concepts. This directly applies to moral reasoning. By using reason alone we infer objective moral rules from the categorical imperative, we make our own moral decisions (judgment) and then we act (will) accordingly. This is the essence of freedom of the will and physical determinism has nothing to do with it. "We must attribute to every being endowed with reason and a will this property of determining itself to action, under the idea of its own freedom" (449).

PART III COMPARISONS, CRITICISMS AND METHOD

7. KANT, PLATO, LOCKE AND MILL

For those who have read the previous three books in the *Smart Student's Guides* series, I am including the following chapters (7, 8 and 9) as a continuation of the series' emphasis on the history of philosophical ethics, philosophical methodology, and important criticisms of the philosopher under scrutiny.

7.1 Plato

Plato, like other ancient philosophers was interested in moral ideals, especially the summum bonum (the greatest good). Plato wrote very little about what constitutes right (just) conduct, although he said a great deal about virtue in general, especially the virtue of justice. The highest aim of conduct is happiness or well-being (eudaimonia), "and the virtues (arête: 'excellence') are the requisite skills and dispositions needed to attain it" (D. Frede).

When Plato wrote about justice in Republic, his objective was to prove that justice could be pursued as something good for itself and not merely good for its consequences. His solution was to show that justice in the individual was a psychological condition in which the rational part of the soul ruled over the appetitive and spirited parts. This is the "natural relation" of mastering and being mastered that is symptomatic of a healthy soul, in which one achieves happiness or well-being (eudaimonia). Injustice, by contrast, is an unnatural relationship in which the appetitive and/or the spirited parts of the soul take over the task of ruling the soul, producing vice, mental disease, and unhappiness.

But Kant would point out (2.1) that under this account, Plato has not shown that justice is good for itself only because Plato has conditioned justice on well-being (the optimum state of the soul). What Plato needs to prove is that justice is unconditionally good, and this he cannot do because justice (as Plato defines it) requires a good will to qualify it as good.

Although it was not Plato's aim to promote a principle of right and wrong, he does attempt to link his account of justice in the soul with just conduct (Republic, 442d-e). Thus, he argues that a person who has justice in the soul would be incapable of committing an unjust act. But Kant would immediately point out that this incapability would depend on the presence of a good will. A person in whom reason is supreme would be just as likely to rob the temple as a person in whom the appetitive part of the soul is supreme, if the former did not have a good will to guide her rational choices.

Despite these differences, it has been argued that Kant's categorical imperative shares with Plato's account of justice the important feature that both are "normative standards for action because they are internal standards of action" (Korsgaard). In this respect, Kant's principle of autonomy of the will (the idea of the will of every rational being as a will that legislates universal law) bears some resemblance to Plato's idea of justice in the soul as determinative of right conduct. But this resemblance would certainly not be enough to persuade Kant that Plato's theory is not heteronomous.

7.2 John Locke

Locke' *Second Treatise of Government* proposes a foundational principle that he calls the law of nature. The law says that "no one ought to harm another in his life, health, liberty or possessions" (§6). Locke identifies law of nature with reason. All that we need to do to confirm the law of nature is to consult reason and we will find that all equal and independent persons have these natural obligations.

Locke's method of consulting reason to discover the law of nature appears to avoid one of Kant's criticisms of other ethical theories. Locke's principle (law) does not appear to be empirical. It is not drawn from "the principle of happiness, [nor is it] based upon either physical or moral feeling" (442).

Is Locke's principle of natural law rational, in Kant's sense of this word? Locke does not spell out what his word "reason" means, nor does he tell his readers how reason can be "consulted" to confirm the law of nature. Perhaps Locke means that the duties specified in the law of nature can be deduced from the equality and independence that persons enjoy in the state of nature. But Locke never explains how we are to get from these two concepts to the law of nature.

When Kant use the word "rational," he means "based upon...the rational concept of perfection as a possible effect of our will" (442). Perfection "exhibits an inevitable tendency for turning about in a circle and cannot avoid tacitly presupposing the morality it has to explain" (442). Locke never uses the word "perfection," but he does appear to be in danger of circularity when suggesting (but not proving) that the law of nature can be derived from the concepts of equality and independence. Equality in the state of nature, for Locke, means moral equality. Two or more persons are morally equally when no one has the right to command the obedience of the others. Independence means being free from (not depending on) the will of any other person when ordering one's actions and disposing of one's person and possessions. But these definitions imply the existence of the very rights which are found in the law of nature. If one is independent and morally equal to all others, then this equality and independence is achieved only when there are moral obligations and rights such as those found in the law of nature. It is the law of nature that guarantees equality and independence, not vice versa.

Although the law of nature cannot stand as the supreme moral principle, it does pass the test of Kant's Categorical Imperative. With respect to each imperative contained in the law of nature, the behavior is prohibited categorically, for example, "Do not harm another in his life." And each imperative can be consistently adopted as a maxim by everyone. Thus, the maxim "Do not harm another in his life" ("in his liberty," "in his health," "in his property") is valid as a universal law.

The end-in-itself formulation (EI) of the categorical imperative also gives support to Locke's law of nature, especially concerning "attacks on the freedom and property of others" (430). Kant classifies the duty not to harm others in their freedom and property as "necessary or strict duties" to others, implying that violations of this duty are violations of another's rights. As such,

> ... a transgressor of the rights of men intends to make use of the persons of others merely as a means, without taking into consideration that, as rational beings, they should always be esteemed at the same time as ends, i.e., be esteemed only as beings who must themselves be able to hold the very same action as an end (430).

Finally, Locke would agree with Kant that a free will must be presumed if human beings are to have a moral law. Locke writes that "the end of law is not to abolish or restrain; but to preserve and enlarge freedom... Where there is no law there is no freedom." Freedom requires an ability to reason because one cannot be "under a law" that is not "promulgated" to him, so that "he that is not come to the use of his reason, cannot be said to be under this law" (Second Treatise, §57). Children are not under the law because lacking understanding, they cannot adjust their behavior to what the law commands. Where there is no freedom there is no law. Hence, freedom for both Locke and Kant is both a necessary and a sufficient condition of a free will.

7.3. John Stuart Mill

John Stuart Mill was born in 1806, about two years after the death of Immanuel Kant. Kant never uses the word "utilitarianism" in his critique of heteronomous principles because this word was not popularized until Mill defended the principle of utility in three magazine articles published in England in 1861.

7.3.1 Hedonism

Those who are acquainted with the hedonist theory of life and John Stuart Mill's defense of it will recall his contention that "happiness is desirable (good) and the only thing desirable as an end" (Util., 35). Kant would agree with Mill that happiness is good, but he would add that it is good only if it is directed by a good will that "corrects its influence on the mind," so that the happy person will not become "prideful and arrogant" (393).

While Mill contends that happiness is the only thing good in itself (as an end), Kant contends that a good will is good in itself "not because of its fitness to attain some proposed end" but "only through its willing" (394).

It is clear that different standards for something being "good in itself" are at play here. Mill is using the standard of a thing being good as an end while Kant is using the standard of being good without qualification. When Mill asserts that happiness is good in itself, he means that it is good as an end not as a means to an end. When Kant asserts that a good will is good in itself, he means that it is good without qualification. When Kant denies that happiness is good in itself, he means that happiness is good only when it is accompanied by a good will.

But what would Mill say about a good will? My guess is that he would not deny that a good will is good as an end in itself. He would probably treat it in the same way that he treated virtue. In his discussion of virtue, Mill said that "the utilitarian doctrine maintains not only that virtue is to be desired, but it is to be desired disinterestedly, for itself" (Util.,36). This initially comes as a surprise to his readers because Mill had previously maintained that happiness is the only thing desired for itself. Mill goes on to explain that "this opinion is not, in the smallest degree, a departure from the happiness principle" because happiness has various "ingredients." One of these ingredients is virtue, and though not naturally and originally a part of happiness, "in those who live it disinterestedly, it has become so, and is desired and cherished, not as a means to happiness, but as a part of their happiness" (17).

A good will might also be promoted by utilitarians as an ingredient or part of happiness. Paraphrasing Mill (by replacing "good will" for the word "virtue"), Mill might say to Kant that utilitarian moralists …[would] recognize as a psychological fact the possibility of a good will being, to the individual, a good in itself, without looking to any end beyond it, and hold that the mind is not in a right state, not in a state conformable to utility, not in the state most conducive to the general happiness, unless it does love a good will in this manner—as a thing desirable in itself…" (16)

This solution is not going to satisfy Kant because he had previously maintained that a good will is good in itself "only through its willing." Mill would probably respond by making the point that willing takes an object. In this respect, willing is like intending. If I say "He had the best of intentions when he tried to please her when he presented her with the gift of roses. How was he to know that she was allergic to roses?!" What makes the man's intention "best" is that it was "to please her." Willing, like intending, must take an object in order to make any sense.

7.3.2 Consequentialist moral principles

The principle of utility is consequentialist. It assumes that right and wrong actions are understood entirely in terms of the consequences produced by the action. What makes the utility principle unique is that the only consequences that count are happiness and the reverse of happiness. "Actions are right in proportion as they tend to produce happiness, wrong as they tend to produce the reverse of happiness. By happiness is intended pleasure and the absence of pain; by unhappiness, pain and the privation of pleasure" (Mill, 7).

Kant would observe that the utility principle is clearly heteronomous, as are all consequentialist principles. An object of the will (happiness or pleasure) is laid down as the foundation for prescribing a rule to determine the will (one ought to tell the truth, keep one's promises). But this makes the imperative hypothetical, viz., if or because one wills the object (happiness), then one should act thus or so (tell the truth, keep one's promises). Hence, the utilitarian imperative does not command morally, i.e., categorically. But a categorical imperative says that "I ought to act this way or that way, even though I did not will something else." Think of it this way: If you tell another that she should tell the truth if this will bring about the most happiness, then you imply that there is no obligation to tell the truth if this does not produce the most happiness. But (Kant would say), there is an obligation to tell the truth independent of any consequences or conditions. Moral principles command categorically, not conditionally. There is no "if" in a moral imperative.

8. OBJECTIONS TO KANT' SUPREME MORAL PRINCIPLE

There are many critical responses to Kantian ethics readily available in the literature (Oxbridge Notes), three of which are mentioned here.

8.1 Failure to exclude immoral rules of conduct

One of the most powerful objections to the categorical imperative came from John Stuart Mill. Although he praised Kant for creating a system of thought that "will long remain one of the landmarks in the history of philosophical speculation," he also remarked that Kant's universal first principle (UL) fails to show that it would be logically impossible for rational beings to universally adopt "the most outrageously immoral rules of conduct." Mill then observes that "all that he shows is that the consequences of their universal adoption would be such as no one would choose to incur" (4).

Unfortunately, Mill does not provide the reader with any examples to back up this charge. So, let's imagine an "outrageously immoral rule of conduct," and see whether the application of Kant's supreme principle (UL) to the rule is one that could be adopted by all rational beings.

Suppose that a man is thinking about raping the woman is he is currently dating. However, he is acquainted with Kant's supreme principle. He has enough conscience to ask himself if the rule "I shall rape a person whenever it would be in my best interest to do so" could be adopted as a law by all rational beings. "Would there be any contradiction, any logical impossibility in the universal adoption of my rule?" Mill's response is that there is no contradiction, or at least none that he can find. "Of course," Mill would be quick to say, "No one would want to see such a rule universally adopted, but this has nothing to do with logical impossibility. It has to do with the overwhelming bad consequences the universal adoption of this outrageous rule would incur."

One response to this objection is to point out that if the rule was universally adopted, it would also apply to this man as a potential rape victim, as well as to everyone else. But this does not show a logical impossibility. It only shows that people would have to significantly alter their behavior to protect themselves from rapists. And once again, it proves Mill's point that we must appeal to utility to show what is "outrageous" about rape and the universal adoption of a rule permitting rape

It was not too long ago that it was not legally wrong nor believed to be morally wrong for a husband to have sexual intercourse with his wife without her consent. The maxim for this behavior would be "A man shall have sexual intercourse with his wife whenever he wishes, even if she does not consent." "Marital rape," as it is called, is now legally prohibited in all U.S. states, and it is generally regarded as morally wrong. But it is not regarded as morally wrong because the preceding maxim logically cannot be adopted by everyone. The maxim does not appear to entail a contradiction.

Let's not forget that Kant has another version of the categorical imperative, not mentioned by Mill, which appears to explain the wrongness of rape. The "end-in-itself" (EI) version of the categorical imperative tells us to treat ourselves, and all others, and ends-in themselves, and never merely as means to an end. I have said (2.5.4 and 2.6) that this is the most popular formulation of the categorical imperative, probably because it shows us exactly why we regard rape as outrageously immoral conduct. To forcibly engage another person in sexual intercourse is to treat her or him as a mere means to an end, in this case, satisfaction of the desire of the rapist. The person who is raped is regarded as a mere tool, a thing, not as a person. Now if it can be shown that EI and UL are morally equivalent, then Kant has the perfect answer to Mill's challenge.

8.2 Conflicting moral rules

A common criticism of Kant and of a priori moralists generally is that his fundamental moral principle does not resolve questions of conflict between moral rules that presumably can be derived from the principle. Kantians can reasonably argue that the Categorical Imperative (CI) and all of its versions were not meant to resolve questions of conflict between duties grounded on CI. CI does not tell us how to rank duties which are categorically imperative. The resolution of real-life moral conflict is a job for practical anthropology (3.1).

The best example of moral conflict is Kant's response to the question about the justification of telling a lie to a person who intends to kill another person who is hiding in your house. The potential murderer appears at your front door and asks the question "Is Jane Doe in your house?" Kant says (categorically) that you ought to tell the truth and say "Yes, she is here." Kant would remind us that the rule about truth-telling is not a hypothetical imperative. It does not say "You ought to tell the truth only if truth-telling will have a good consequence." It says (categorically), "Tell the truth."

But there is another moral rule mentioned by Kant that can also be applied to this case. It is the imperative that tells us to help others (whom we can help) by giving them assistance when they are struggling with great hardships. This rule, like the rule on truth-telling, is endorsed by the categorical imperative in that the universal adoption of its opposite (not giving help to others in need) is practically impossible for us to will as a universal law (2.5.3.3). Thus, when the man with murderous intent arrives at your front door, and asks you if Jane

Doe is in your house, the imperative to help others in distress morally compels you to tell the man the lie that she is not in your house.

Suppose you are the one who is hiding in the house. To paraphrase Kant, a will which resolved to tell the truth in a case such as this "would contradict itself, inasmuch as cases like this might often arise in which you would have need of the love and sympathy of others and in which you would deprive yourself, by such a law of nature springing from your own will, of all hope of the aid you want for yourself" (423) (See "a contradiction in willing" at 5.5.5.3).

While Kantians struggle with dilemmas like this, utilitarians come to the rescue with the greatest happiness principle. It is obvious that the act that would promote the greatest happiness is to save the life of the innocent person by telling a lie about her whereabouts. Utilitarians would call this case a "slam dunk" for their side of the debate. Although it is true that the would-be murderer experiences frustration, this consequence does not begin to compare with the happiness experienced by his would-be victim and her friends and family as a consequence of having told the lie, thereby thwarting the murderer's plan.

8.3 Confusing the motive of action with the rule of action

Some philosophers argue that there is a clear distinction between the question "Did you do the morally right act?" and "Are you a morally good person?" The motive for what you did has nothing to do with the former question, but it has much to do with the latter. If you jumped fully clothed into the swimming pool and rescued a child from drowning, you did the morally right thing no matter what your motive might have been. It does not matter whether you acted from duty, instinct, inclination, or in the hope of getting a substantial reward from the child's parents. If motive matters at all, then it would matter only if we are uncertain about whether you are a good person. If you admit that you rescued the child only to collect a reward, then we might judge you to be less praiseworthy you than if you had said "I cannot bear to witness human suffering," or "We all have an obligation to help one another in times of distress."

If it is true that motive is irrelevant to a determination of right and wrong, then Kant's insistence on acting from the motive of duty is brought into question. One can do the right thing (rescuing a child) from a questionable motive (to collect a reward), even if others will think less about your character. In general, it might be argued that we would prefer that people do the right thing from motives that have nothing to do with "duty" than that they defer from doing the right thing at all.

Of course, none of this will persuade a Kantian who will insist that the consequences of what we do have no bearing on whether what we do is right or wrong

.

9. PHILOSOPHICAL METHOD

Kant tells us in the preface to *Grounding* that his method is to proceed "analytically from common knowledge to the determination of its ultimate principle." The common knowledge to which he refers is found in his remarks about "a good will," that is, that the only thing which can be called good, without qualification, is a good will. Thus, by the mere contemplation of the concept of a good will we should be able to eventually deduce the categorical imperative by moving analytically from a good will to actions done from duty, and from this to actions done out of respect for law as such (that is, the Categorical Imperative).

The progression has already been described in 5.7 where Kant states that "we can now end where we started at the beginning, viz., the concept of an unconditionally good will." The categorical imperative (UL) is not only analytically implied by the concept of a good will, but the concept of a good will analytically implies the categorical imperative.

In this analytical task, Kant insists that the principles of morality are never to be sought in human nature because moral knowledge cannot be acquired a posteriori, by experience. This approach makes the principles derived therefrom heteronomous and thereby should be cast aside as "spurious principles of morality." Moral principles must be found altogether "a priori, free from everything empirical, in pure rational concepts only" (411). Any principle which contains something empirical is not a moral principle. Moral principles inform us categorically about our moral duty. But empirical principles can only command conditionally or hypothetically.

Unless you are prepared to argue with Kant about his wholesale rejection of heteronomous ethical theories, the only way to react critically is either to show that some or all of Kant's a priori deductions are invalid or present him with an alternative ethical theory based entirely on "rational concepts only." In the vast literature on the ethical writings of Immanuel Kant, you will find many examples of both kinds of critiques.

What is most important about Kant's methodology is that it strictly adheres to the fundamental rules of logic. This is evident throughout the Grounding, for example his use of a valid deductive form to prove that the categorical imperative presupposes an end (5.5.4) or his use of counterexamples to prove that the Golden Rule does not qualify as a universal law (5.5.5.2). Kant does not appeal to the gods, to mystical revelation, or to Biblical passages to support his claims. In this respect his methods do not differ from most Western philosophers. Although his rationalist assumptions about how to justify a proposed moral principle are different from those of the so-called empirical school of ethics, John Stuart Mill is right in his observation that both he and Kant agree that "there is a science of morals," and that "morality must be deduced from principles" (Util, 3).

The word "science" means that philosophers can hypothesize moral principles as objectively valid and then put them to the test by attempting to deduce morality from these principles. If the deduction fails, then it is back to the drawing board. But this is the essence of philosophy – its greatest virtue is that it teaches us not what to think, but how to think.

GLOSSARY

A posteriori -- Knowledge that is dependent on or derived from experience

A priori -- Knowledge that is independent of all particular experiences

Absolute necessity -- Logical necessity or true by definition, as in "Triangles have three sides"

Absolute value -- Unconditioned or intrinsic value, as opposed to instrumental value.

Analytic -- Judgments in which the predicate is contained in the subject, as in "Bachelors are unmarried adult males." See synthetic.

Autonomy of the will -- The capacity to deliberate and give the moral law to oneself.

Categorical imperative -- A command that represents an action as "objectively necessary in itself, without reference to another end" as in "Thou shalt always tell the truth." See *hypothetical*.

Contradiction in thinking A contradiction that occurs when it is logically impossible to universalize a maxim (e.g. the maxim "I shall make a false promise whenever it suits my purposes")

Contradiction in willing -- A contradiction that occurs when the universalization of a maxim commands (wills) conduct that might have an unwanted (unwilled) effect on the one doing the willing (e.g. "I shall never help others in need").

Deduction --To deduce a moral principle is to justify it.

Dignity -- The inner, unconditional worth of the moral law.

Duty -- To act from duty is to act from respect for the moral law, as opposed to acting from some other motive, for example the hope of favor from others.

Empiricism -- In ethics, empiricism is the theory that moral principles are ultimately derived from observation and experience of human behavior. See *inductive school*.

End in itself -- As opposed to being treated by others or even by oneself as a mere "means to an end." See formula of the end in itself.

Eudaemonism -- The doctrine that happiness or well-being is the highest good.

False promising -- Promising to do something when one intends or foresees that he or she will not keep the promise (also known as a *lying promise*)

Formula of autonomy -- A version of the categorical imperative that proclaims, "the idea of the will of every rational being as a will that legislates universal law." ("All principles are rejected which are not consistent with the will's own legislation of universal law").

Formula of humanity -- See *formula of the end.*

Formula of the end -- A version of the categorical imperative that says, "Act in such a way that you treat humanity, whether in your own person or in the person of another, always at the same time as an end and never simply as a means."

Formula of universal law -- This is Kant's first version of the categorical imperative: "Act only according to that maxim whereby you can at the same time will that it should become a universal law."

Free will -- A free will is identical with autonomy, that is, the property of being a law to itself.

Good will -- A will that is good only through its willing, i.e., it is good in itself.

Good with qualification -- Something that is good because of what it effects or accomplishes, or because of its fitness to attain some proposed end.

Happiness -- An indeterminate concept, such that one can never say definitely what it is that he wishes and wills when he wishes and wills happiness. This is because all the elements of happiness are borrowed from experience.

Heteronomy of the will --The property of a will that seeks the law to determine it outside of itself in the character of any of its objects (for example, inclination or self-interest). See *autonomy of the will.*

Hypothetical imperative -- Imperatives are hypothetical when they represent the practical necessity of a possible action as a means for attaining something else that one wants (or may possibly want).

Inductive school – Those who believe in a theory of ethics maintaining that "right and wrong, as well as truth and falsehood, are questions of observation and experience" (J.S. Mill).

Intuitive school – Those who believe in a theory of ethics maintaining that the principles of morals are "evident a priori, requiring nothing to command assent except that the meaning of the terms be understood" (J.S. Mill).

Kingdom of ends -- A version of the categorical imperative that says, "Act in such a way that one is a member of a systematic union of rational beings, where he legislates in universal laws while also being himself subject to these laws."

Law -- Commands which must be obeyed, that is, must be followed even in opposition to inclination.

Maxim -- The subjective principle of volition,

Metaphysics of morals -- A philosophy which sets forth its doctrines as founded entirely on a priori principles or determinate objects (concepts) of the understanding.

Moral law -- A law that carries with it absolute necessity and is valid as a ground of obligation.

Moral worth -- An action has moral worth only when it is done from the motive of duty.

Popular philosophy -- Dealing in moral philosophy in a way favored by popular taste.

Rational agent -- A being who is capable of the idea of pure practical reason and can be given a priori laws, unaffected by human inclinations.

Respect – In the context of respect for the law, respect occurs when the law is connected to the will solely as ground and never as effect—it does not serve my inclination, but rather outweighs it.

Synthetic -- Judgments in which the predicate says more than what is contained in the subject, as in "Bachelors are less than twenty feet tall." See analytic.

Synthetic a priori -- A synthetic judgment that is known to be true a priori. For example, "Every event has a cause."

Universalizability test -- Using the categorical imperative to determine whether a maxim can be willed as a universal law.

Will -- A faculty of choosing only that which reason, independently of inclination, recognizes as being practically necessary, that is, as good. Hence, the will is nothing but practical reason.

REFERENCES

Allison, Henry E., 2011. Kant's Groundwork for the Metaphysics of Morals: A Commentary. Oxford University Press. http://www.oxfordscholarship.com/view/10.1093/acprof:oso/9780199 691531.001.0001/acprof-9780199691531. Retrieved 10 Aug. 2018.

Coffa, J., 1991, The Semantic Tradition from Kant to Carnap: to the Vienna Station, Cambridge: Cambridge University Press. 2015

Denis, Lara and Oliver Sensen. 2015. Kant's Lectures on Ethics: A Critical Guide. Cambridge University Press.

Dillon, Robin S. 2018. "Respect", The Stanford Encyclopedia of Philosophy, Edward N. Zalta (ed.), URL = <https://plato.stanford.edu/archives/spr2018/entries/respect/>.

Ellington, James W., 1981 and 1993. (trans.) Immanuel Kant, Grounding for the Metaphysics of Morals. Cambridge: Hackett..

Frede, Dorothea. 2017. "Plato's Ethics: An Overview", The Stanford Encyclopedia of Philosophy Edward N. Zalta (ed.). https://plato.stanford.edu/archives/win2017/entries/plato-ethics

Houlgate, Laurence. 2016. Understanding Plato: The Smart Student's Guide to the Socratic Dialogues and the Republic. Amazon Kindle.

Houlgate, Laurence. 2017. Understanding John Locke: The Smart Student's Guide to Second Treatise of Government.

Houlgate, Laurence. 2018. Understanding John Stuart Mill: The Smart Student's Guide to Utilitarianism and On Liberty, Amazon Kindle.

Hume, David, 1738 [1975]. A Treatise of Human Nature, ed. L.A. Selby-Bigge, rev. P.H. Nidditch, Oxford: Clarendon Press.

Jachmann, Reinhold Bernhard. 1804. Immanuel Kant geschildert in Briefen an einen Freund. Konigsberg: F. Nicolovius. Trans. Robert B. Loudon.

Kant, I., 1781 [1998], The Critique of Pure Reason, P. Guyer and A.W. Wood (trans.), Cambridge: Cambridge University Press.

_____. 1785 and 1799 [1993], Grounding for the Metaphysics of Morals and On a Supposed Right to Lie because of Philanthropic Concerns J.W. Ellington (trans). Cambridge: Hackett.

_____. 1785 [2012]. Groundwork for the Metaphysics of Morals. Edited and translated by Mary Gregor and Jens Timmerman. New York: Cambridge University Press.

Korsgaard, Christine. 2008. "Self-Constitution in the Ethics of Plato and Kant" in Christine Korsgaard (ed.) The Constitution of Agency: Essays on Practical Reason and Moral Psychology. Oxford: Oxford University Press
.

Mill, J.S. 1861 [2001]. Utilitarianism. G. Sher (ed. 2nd edition). Indianapolis: Hackett Publishing Co.

Morongowiusz, Kryxztof. 1784-85.[1992]. Mrongrovious II: A Supplement to the Groundwork of the Metaphysics of Morals. Paul

Guyer and Allen Wood (eds.). Cambridge Edition of the Writings of Immanuel Kant. (Cambridge University Press).

Oxbridge Notes. 2010-2018. Objections and Problems to Kant's Ethics. https://www.oxbridgenotes.co.uk/

Rey, Georges, "The Analytic/Synthetic Distinction", The Stanford Encyclopedia of Philosophy (Fall 2018 Edition), Edward N. Zalta (ed.), https://plato.stanford.edu/archives/fall2018/entries/analytic-synthetic/

Scruton, Roger. 2001. Kant: A Very Short Introduction. Oxford. Oxford University Press.

ABOUT LAURENCE HOULGATE

Laurence Houlgate is Emeritus Professor of Philosophy at California Polytechnic State University in San Luis Obispo, California. He received M.A. and Ph.D. degrees in philosophy at the University of California, Los Angeles. Prior to joining the Cal Poly faculty in 1979 he held professorships at the University of California, Santa Barbara, and George Mason University. In addition to the books in the *Smart Student's Guide* series, he has published four books on the ethics and law of family relationships and many journal articles on moral and legal responsibility. He lives in San Luis Obispo with his wife Torre and when he is not writing, he enjoys genealogy, philately and swimming.